The Great War, 1914–1918

THE GREAT WAR, 1914–1918

The Cartoonists' Vision

ROY DOUGLAS

London and New York

First published 1995
by Routledge
11 New Fetter Lane, London EC4P 4EE

Simultaneously published in the USA and Canada
by Routledge
29 West 35th Street, New York, NY 10001

©1995 Roy Douglas

Typeset in 10 on 12 point Sabon by
Florencetype Ltd, Stoodleigh, Devon

Printed and bound in Great Britain by
TJ Press (Padstow) Ltd, Padstow, Cornwall

British Library Cataloguing in Publication Data
A catalogue record for this book is available from the British Library

Library of Congress Cataloguing in Publication Data
A catalogue record for this book has been requested

ISBN 0–415–117135

Contents

Acknowledgements		vii
Introduction		1
1	The outbreak of war	5
2	The war develops	12
3	New ways of waging war	20
4	Mediterranean dramas, 1915	27
5	Changing patterns	35
6	War in the East, 1915	44
7	War for its own sake	53
8	The smaller nations, 1916	60
9	Peace moves, 1916–17	69
10	Revolution in Russia: stage 1	79
11	America enters the war	85
12	A time of waiting	93
13	Revolution in Russia: stage 2	102
14	Revolution in Russia: stage 3	108
15	The last throw	122
16	Collapse, 1918	128
17	Aftermath	136
18	A sort of peace	145

Acknowledgements

The author wishes to thank those who have helped with this book. As usual, he expresses his grateful thanks to his wife Jean, who read and criticised the manuscript. He also wishes to thank those who criticised his translations: Professor Bertram Pockney and Mr John Taylor of the University of Surrey, and Mr David K. Mills. Several useful ideas were generated in these criticisms, which have been incorporated in the book.

The author would also like to thank the suppliers of the material from which the cartoons were drawn, particularly the British Library (including the Newspaper Library), and the University of Kent at Canterbury.

Introduction

It is difficult for the modern reader who knows something of the conditions under which the 'Great War' of 1914–18 was fought, to appreciate why people went on fighting that war for four years, and did not discover some way of bringing it to an earlier end. The leading statesmen of both sides, as well as ordinary people, had plenty of reason for doing so.

Before one can attempt an answer to this and other questions about the Great War, it is important to recall the old cliché that there are at least two sides to any question. When the 'question' is a great international conflict, there are usually a great many more than two sides. Each national government, belligerent or neutral, has its own side; for no two allies ever have identical interests. Within each government, and between the people of each country, there are usually various sides. To understand attitudes to a conflict, and the general course of that conflict, it is necessary to appreciate the existence, and the opinions, of all the 'sides'.

Cartoons cast important light on why people on all sides were prepared to go on fighting, and also on the various points of view which were expressed as the war proceeded. Cartoons usually encapsulate arguments. Those arguments tell us much about the atmosphere of the time. They may seem stupid or dishonest today but they evidently struck home to the people who saw the cartoons when they were originally produced. Some of those points of view were largely forgotten when the victors came to write the history of the conflict in the light of after-knowledge.

In the present book, the author has drawn together cartoons from the Great War from many different national sources, in the hope and belief that they show much of the social and political assumptions of the time. Some of these assumptions are still held in certain quarters today, but they are all a good deal less universal than they were in the second decade of the twentieth century.

One of the most important of these ideas was the view that Europe was of overriding importance in all international dealings. Nearly all of Africa and Australasia, a very large part of Asia, and a considerable part of the Americas was dominated by Powers whose centres of government were situated in Europe. Cartoons from non-European countries uphold

1

this point of view. American cartoons from the early phase of the war suggest that the United States was essentially a spectator rather than a participant in great events; while throughout the war most cartoons from British Dominions support the view that the people of those countries saw themselves essentially as expatriate Britons, even though they also felt a sense of developing nationhood, which the war itself helped to encourage.

Among the Europeans themselves, there was a precarious balance between six or seven 'Great Powers'. What made a country a Great Power was not so much its capacity to wage war, or the area which it governed, or the economic muscle it possessed, but rather the disposition of other Great Powers to acknowledge that it had a kind of right to be consulted on matters which seemed important to its statesmen.

Britain, France, Germany and Russia were Great Powers in the fullest sense of the term, with massive possessions, conjoined with economic and military strength. Austria–Hungary and Italy also ranked as Great Powers, although they were considerably weaker than the other four. The Ottoman Empire, or Turkey, was also generally treated as a Great Power, although quite recent events had cast considerable doubt as to whether she still merited that status.

Other ideas prevalent in the early twentieth century are also important in understanding attitudes which existed during the Great War. The idea of 'nationalism' – the idea that people of one nation are morally or even biologically superior to those of all other nations – was widely held, and many cartoons take nationalism more or less for granted. Nationalism implied that the interests of members of a nation were much closer than the interests of people linked together in other ways: because they shared a political ideology, for example; or because they belonged to the same social class.

But what is a 'nation'? It was easy to give a rough definition of the French nation, for example, as those people who lived in France, or who spoke French as their first language, or who thought of themselves as French. Even those three senses of the French 'nation' were not identical. For example, some people living in France did not speak French as their first language, and quite a lot of people living outside France did speak French as their first language.

The further east one moved in Europe, the more difficult it became to decide just what a nation was. What nations were encompassed in the Austro–Hungarian Empire? Did a citizen of the Empire whose first language was German belong to the Austro–Hungarian or the German nation? Which of the South Slavs within the Empire belonged properly to the Serbian nation? In 1915, when war broke out between the Empire and Italy, to which nation did a citizen of the Empire who spoke Italian properly owe allegiance?

There were innumerable difficulties of that kind and the various belligerents were often eager to exploit them. Russians were glad to encourage Czechs towards the view that they had closer affinities with Russia than they had with the Austro–Hungarian Empire in which they were currently included; while Austrians and Germans encouraged Poles living in the Russian Empire to the view that they had no affinities at all with the Russian nation, Britons encouraged Arabs living in the Ottoman Empire to think of themselves as belonging to a completely different nation from the Turks who dominated the Empire; while Germans encouraged Irish people to take a corresponding view of their relationship with the United Kingdom. Some of the cartoons in this book show ways in which these conflicting appeals to nationalism were made.

In all European countries, society was a good deal more hierarchical in 1914 than it is today. This made it easy to believe that blame or praise attributable to the leaders also applied to all members of the society. Most Britons and Frenchmen, for example, believed that the German Emperor was wicked. Many of them derived from that proposition the view that all Germans were tainted by his wickedness, and it was therefore moral and reasonable that they should be punished. Similarly, most Britons and Frenchmen considered that the King of the Belgians was brave, and therefore that all Belgian people basked, as it were, in the sunshine of his bravery. These ideas are frequently found in cartoons of the Allied (sometimes known as the *entente*) countries. Corresponding, but different, ideas are found in cartoons of the opposing countries, who were usually known as the Central Powers. All Russians shared in the infamy of the Tsar. The Italian government was seen to have behaved treacherously towards Germany and Austria–Hungary in 1915, so all Italians shared this moral obloquy.

Yet, paradoxically, many people were disposed to excuse their own nation (or perhaps one should say their government) from any sort of duty under moral law in dealings either with its own subjects, or, *a fortiori*, with other nations. 'Act of State' was a complete defence for any crime. This idea is also frequently found in cartoons.

Something must be said about the background to the war of 1914. From time to time there had been wars between Great Powers; but from the final defeat of Napoleon in 1815 down to the outbreak of war in 1914 there was no European war which involved killing or material destruction on a scale remotely comparable with that of the two so-called 'World Wars' of the twentieth century. From 1815 to 1914, Great Powers had seldom, or never, sought the utter extinction of other Great Powers.

For much of the nineteenth century, people frequently spoke of the Concert of Europe – a term which implied that the European Great Powers, despite their differences, were conscious that there was much more to unite them than to divide them. Great Powers summoned Congresses whenever there seemed to be a serious risk of general war breaking out. What emerged from the various Congresses was some kind of arrangement, or string of arrangements, which did not do too much violence to the interests of any of the Great Powers.

Towards the end of the nineteenth century, people gradually stopped talking of the Concert of Europe, and ceased to envisage general Congresses as the means of solving serious disputes. Alliances between Great Powers became increasingly the order of the day. There was the Triple Alliance between Germany and Austria–Hungary, with Italy more loosely attached, and there was the Dual Alliance between France and Russia. Yet it is noteworthy that both of those Alliances were essentially defensive in character. Neither of them required a member-country to go to war unless a partner was attacked by someone else.

Britain remained outside both Alliances. In the early twentieth century she had concluded *ententes* with France and Russia, but these were, in form at least, merely the resolution of past points of disagreement. Neither *entente* carried any obligation on any party to go to war in support of the other in any circumstances at all; nor did it prohibit the parties from making similar *ententes* with other countries. In practice, however, the *ententes* moved Britain decisively towards the Franco-Russian side, Soon she was involved in serious rivalry with Germany, particularly in naval affairs, and ordinary people in both countries came to see the other as a kind of 'moral enemy'.

Yet, despite these important considerations which seemed to be disposing Europe towards war, the last two or three years of peace witnessed a gradual return to stability. To that point it will be necessary to return in the first chapter.

1

The outbreak of war

In studying the outbreak of war in 1914, it is very easy to miss the wood for the trees: to know so much of the detail of who did what to whom, when and why, that the outline becomes lost in a mass of detail. Thus, much has been said about entangling alliances as a cause of the 1914 war. Those alliances certainly determined the orientation of some of the Powers in the conflict, but it is striking to note that no Great Powers entered the war because of obligations imposed by an alliance.

One point which emerges with reasonable certainty is that nobody of importance anywhere intended, or even contemplated, a conflict like the one which actually took place. This applies equally to governments, to military leaders, to commercial and business classes, and to ordinary people in the belligerent countries. Even the armaments manufacturers had not planned for the kinds of weapons which were actually in principal demand in that kind of war. Pictures of jubilant crowds in the various national capitals suggest that a substantial proportion of the various populations anticipated a brief period of high adventure, followed by a convincing triumph.

A matter which will require constant attention in this study is the way in which the major issues of the war looked profoundly different in different places. Austria–Hungary was deeply concerned over Serbia, which was of much less interest to Germany, of minimal interest to France and of no interest at all to Britain. Most Britons would have been hard put to find Serbia on a map. French antagonism towards Germany probably owed more to the question of Alsace and Lorraine than to any other. Britain was deeply interested in Belgium; yet the German Chancellor was expressing honest puzzlement rather than cynicism in his famous aphorism about Britain going to war for a 'scrap of paper'. To Germany, the overwhelming matter of concern at the outbreak of war was not Belgium or Serbia, Britain or France, but Russia. The Russians were probably as mystified as everybody else, and doubtless saw their position as one of purest defence against unprovoked attacks. They can hardly have viewed either Belgium or Serbia or, for that matter, Britain or France as much more than peripheral. To people in Japan, all the conflicts in Europe must have seemed remote. By contrast, many people in British Dominions, who were equally distant geographically from the main fighting, simply thought of Britain as 'home', and identified almost automatically with what seemed to them to be Britain's cause.

Motives of the various Powers have been interpreted and re-interpreted ever since the war began. David Thomson, the author of *Europe Since Napoleon* (1978), was not far wrong when he wrote that 'Fear, rather than greed or idealism, dominated the decisions of all the powers in 1914'. The confusion of the time is such that in several cases there is dispute between apparently competent authorities over exact dates; but the sequence, stated rather flatly, runs approximately as follows.

On 28 June 1914, Franz Ferdinand, heir presumptive to the Austro–Hungarian empire, was assassinated at Sarajevo, in Bosnia, by a Serbian subject of the empire. There seems little reason today for thinking that the Serbian government was directly responsible for the crime, although it seemed otherwise to people at the time. Some highly placed Serbs may have known what was plotted, and Serbia's general hostility to Austria–Hungary was not in doubt.

Nearly four weeks later, on 23 July, an ultimatum was presented by Austria–Hungary to Serbia, requiring the Serbs to make various humiliating concessions. Within the time prescribed, Serbia accepted most, but not all, of the demands, and requested international arbitration on the remainder. Austria–Hungary appears to have regarded this as a mere tactic to gain time, and on 28 July declared war. Minor incursions took place in both directions, but there was no general fighting between Austria–Hungary and Serbia until several Great Powers were already involved.

On 31 July, although already technically at war, Austria–Hungary intimated that she would consent to mediation on the Serbian question, but on the same day she ordered general mobilisation. Russia appears to have decided at an early stage that Austria–Hungary was deeply hostile to herself. Despite this, her initial attitude to Serbia was to counsel moderation. On 29 July, however, Russia responded to the Austro–Hungarian declaration of war on Serbia by declaring partial mobilisation.

Austria–Hungary was then placed in a very difficult position, for purely technical reasons: it was impossible to mobilise first against Serbia and later against Russia should events so require. And so, on 31 July, the Dual Monarchy ordered general mobilisation, which affected the frontier with Russia as well as the frontier with Serbia. On the same day Russia, no doubt considering herself directly threatened, also ordered general mobilisation.

That mobilisation also applied along the Russian frontier with Germany. It provoked an almost immediate German ultimatum, demanding Russian demobilisation. On 1 August, Germany declared war on Russia; the first outbreak of war between Great Powers. Strikingly, war was not declared between Austria–Hungary and Russia until five days later.

On 1 August, France mobilised. Germany sought to discover whether France proposed to remain neutral. The overriding German concern was to avoid a two-front war, for which France might choose her own moment. On 3 August, when the French had refused to give a clear answer to the German question, Germany declared war on France, hoping to knock out France quickly, and then turn to face Russia. Considerations of strategy suggested to Germany that the most effective way of doing this was to strike at northern France through Belgium. Accordingly, Germany sought right of passage through Belgium, promising as an inducement that Belgian integrity would otherwise be respected, and that compensation would be paid after the war for any damage done by German troops. Belgium refused, and on 4 August Germany invaded.

While war between Germany and France was becoming increasingly likely, a great debate had raged in the British Cabinet as to whether Britain should intervene in support of France. The attack on Belgium swung most of the waverers. On 4 August, Britain issued an ultimatum against Germany. When this was rejected, war was declared. Two members of the Liberal Cabinet resigned, although in neither case was the reason stated on clearly anti-war grounds. Within a very short time all United Kingdom parties, including the Irish Nationalists, indicated support for the prosecution of war, although a few Liberal and Labour MPs demurred for more or less pacifist reasons.

And so, in just over a week from the Austro–Hungarian declaration of war on Serbia, five Great Powers were at war, as well as the much smaller countries of Serbia, Montenegro and Belgium.

Cartoon 1.1 The Avalanche, *New York Tribune,* New York, 9.viii.1914

THE AVALANCHE.

Franz Josef—I didn't know this little one was a keystone.

This American cartoon, which appeared shortly after the war had involved five European Great Powers, represents a fairly typical neutral view. Franz Josef has just pulled out the little rock Serbia, not appreciating the importance of what he was doing. The avalanche has started.

This cartoon, like most foreign drawings and many British ones of the period, fails to distinguish between England, Britain and the United Kingdom.

Cartoon 1.2 Auf deutsche Brüder . . . *Kladderadatsch*, Berlin, 9.viii.1914

The young man in this cartoon is cast as a tribesman at the time of the fifth-century invasions, warning his 'German brothers' that the Huns have arrived, but the allusion is intended to be contemporary. The Russians are seen as the Huns.

The invasion of Attila's Huns was effectively broken at the battle of Châlons in 451 by a combination of Romans and Germanic barbarians. The word 'Hun' acquired particular terror in many minds, and it is striking that it was widely used in Britain to refer to Germans, while the Germans themselves are here applying it to Russians. Both usages are historically and ethnically false. The Huns were an Asian people whose contribution to either German or European Russian bloodstock was minimal.

The real significance of this cartoon is the light it casts on German attitudes at the outbreak of war in 1914. At that date, many Germans were deeply fearful of the impending Russian invasion of their own country, for they often perceived Russians as little better than savages. In Germany, as in the Allied countries, there was a more or less spontaneous, and nearly complete, 'national unity' at the beginning of the war. To Germans, the overwhelming issue was the perceived Russian threat to their own country.

9

Cartoon 1.3 Bravo, Belgium! *Punch*, London, 12.viii.1914

BRAVO, BELGIUM!

In this famous British cartoon, the hero who invites the reader's sympathy is a modern Belgian peasant, not an ancient warrior. The Belgian stands in defence of his village against the bigger German with his huge cudgel. The association of the German with his pipe and sausages would have been recognised at once by the 1914 reader.

In this cartoon, as in the preceding German one, the theme is one on which 'national unity' was practically complete. Just as Germans who might have felt doubts about fighting Frenchmen had no hesitation about resisting a Russian invasion, so also did Britons, who would have had considerable hesitation about taking arms to support France or Russia, feel deep admiration for 'gallant little Belgium's' stand against the German attack.

Cartoon 1.4 Nailing it to the Mast. *Daily Star*, Montreal, 10.viii.1914

NAILING IT TO THE MAST.

A few nails to help the old man nail it tighter, and plenty more if he wants them.

This cartoon appeared in a Canadian newspaper circulating in Quebec, the least 'British' province. The young Canadian offers 'a few nails' – a contingent of 20,000 men – to help 'the old man' – his father, the British sailor – to nail the Union Jack to the mast.

Under the constitutional doctrine of 'Unity of the Crown' which prevailed in 1914 (although not in 1939), the British declaration of war automatically involved the whole British Empire, including the self-governing Dominions. There was little doubt, however, that in most of the Dominions support was genuine and spontaneous – not so much because of special issues like Belgium, but because the people thought of themselves as British.

2

The war develops

Two important countries soon entered the contest, each of its own volition, but on opposite sides. Japan joined the Allies on 23 August, while Turkey joined the enemy Central Powers during the autumn.

The war quickly took on a character which none had foreseen, but which it was to retain for a very long time to come.

The course of military operations in Europe rapidly dispelled the original idea that the war would be one of swift strategic movements. The German Schlieffen Plan, which had been designed to knock out France by a massive attack through Belgium, encountered stiffer resistance than had been anticipated. The small, but very highly trained, British Expeditionary Force seems to have played an important part in this operation, and the French were able to counter-attack to great effect. By the late autumn, most of Belgium and a substantial part of north-eastern France were in German hands, but the attempted knock-out blow had visibly failed. Thereafter, both sides settled into a phase of trench warfare which was to last for years.

On the eastern front, it was Russia who took the initial offensive. In the first couple of months large advances were made against Austria-Hungary in Galicia, but the great assault against Germany in East Prussia was held and thrown back. By the end of the year the Eastern Front, like the Western, had settled down in a pattern of stagnation and attrition. Even the Southern Front, between Austria-Hungary and Serbia, developed in a similar way. An Austrian attack at first threatened to overwhelm Serbia; then the Serbians rallied and counter-attacked, but they too were held and the front stabilised.

At sea the Allies had the inital advantage, but the German navy, though kept mainly in port, remained a very powerful threat. The Allies were able to commence a blockade against ships bound for German ports, while Germany's incapacity to supply her overseas empire encouraged various successful assaults, including some by Japan and by the British Dominions. The German overseas empire, however, was by no means extinct at the end of 1914, and parts of it survived right to the end of the war. A rebellion by disaffected Boers in South Africa provided some embarrassment for the Dominion government, but it was beaten down before 1914 came to an end.

Thus by the latter part of 1914 it was evident that no great change would take place, except at enormous cost. The brief wars of the period 1859–71, or even the Balkan wars of 1912–13, which had achieved massive political results at relatively low human and material cost, would not be repeated. Nor indeed was it very clear what positive war aims any of the major European belligerents entertained. If it had been possible for the governments of the Great Powers to view matters objectively, they would probably have decided that there was everything to be said for some sort of compromise peace, comparable with the arrangements made by the Congresses of Berlin in 1878, and Paris in 1856.

This, however, was out of the question. Popular passions had been stirred up everywhere. Even if the statesmen had been able to take a cool view, they would not have been able to control the feelings which had been unleashed among their peoples. Whatever their private reservations might have been, they were compelled to act as if they believed that the next great military operation would bring complete victory.

Cartoon 2.1 Japan hilf! *Kladderadatsch,* Berlin, 13.ix.1914

Da Marianne mit Schrecken die Ohnmacht ihrer europäischen Götzen bemerkt, so betet sie jetzt die asiatischen an.

This German cartoon, 'Help, Japan!', commemorates Japan's entry to the war on the Allied side. Although there was an Anglo-Japanese agreement dating from 1902, it is difficult to see how this imposed any obligation upon Japan in the existing circumstances. However, Japan sought to acquire German colonies and areas of influence in the Pacific region.

Marianne and President Raymond Poincaré of France move desperately from altar to altar in quest of divine assistance. In the centre, a figure representing Britain shows damaged limbs. The Russian bear to the right is also powerless to assist; for the hand bearing the knout which was associated with internal repression in Russia has broken off. The two French figures now grovel before the savage-looking Japanese idol. As the text observes, their European gods have let them down, so they now turn to an Asian one. A German soldier, sword in hand, seeks out the worshippers.

14

Cartoon 2.2 L'Alliance Germano–Turque.
Le Charivari, Paris, 22.xi.1914

L'ALLIANCE GERMANO-TURQUE

Qui se ressemblent s'assemblent.

This French cartoon commemorates Turkey's entry to the war on Germany's side in November 1914.

The caption might be rendered idiomatically as 'birds of a feather flock together'. To the left of the picture, the German and the Turk are both pictured as pyromaniacs. The right side of the picture suggests that both indulge in physical torture. The German officer beats his recruit; the Turk strikes the soles of the feet of the fettered prisoner.

Cartoon 2.3 Pa Okhote. *Novoe Vremya*, St Petersburg, 27.ix/10.x.1914

In the autumn of 1914, the Russians invading eastern Prussia had sustained massive defeat, but their armies entering Galicia, in the Austro-Hungarian Empire, were far more successful.

The Russian cartoonist notes the victory, but ignores the defeat. The German and the Austrian are, as the title indicates, 'on the hunt'. They have come upon a gigantic and angry Russian bear. The German impels the Austrian forward, protesting that the bear is advancing.

Cartoon 2.4 Der Conquerors. *The Bulletin,* Sydney, 10.x.1914

DER CONQUERORS.

German Samoa, it is officially announced, has surrendered to the British forces. The occupation was effected quietly.

THE COLONIST : *"Hoch der — Gott sag."*

Much of the German overseas empire was conquered by the Allies at a very early stage of the war, although some of it held until the end. This Australian cartoon commemorates victory in the German colony of Western Samoa, which was captured by New Zealand forces, with support from Australian, British and French naval vessels, in the first month of war.

Cartoon 2.5 On the Veldt. *Westminster Gazette*, London, 2.xi.1914

ON THE VELDT.

THE LION AND THE WILD BOER.

This cartoon appeared in the *Westminster Gazette*, a newspaper of Liberal views circulating mainly in London. As the Liberal government had given South Africa what would now be called 'Dominion status' in 1910, it had a special interest in events in that country.

In South Africa, support for the Allied cause was a good deal weaker than it was in the other Dominions. South African opponents of the war were heavily defeated in the Union's House of Assembly, but soon afterwards some Boers actually took to the field against the Government. In this cartoon the lion bears the features of the South African Prime Minister, General Hertzog – a Boer, but also a strong supporter of the Allied cause. Hertzog defends the 'South African Union', but is defied by the 'wild Boer', Christian De Wet. The poignancy of the cartoon is that De Wet and Hertzog had both fought as Boer officers against the British in the South African War of 1899–1902. As in the conflict at the turn of the century, puns on Boer–boar–bore were tediously frequent.

The Boer rising was foredoomed from the start, but provided a considerable embarrassment to the Allies. It did not finally collapse until early 1915.

Cartoon 2.6 Die Spionenfurcht in London.
Simplicissimus, Munich, 10.xi.1914

Die Spionenfurcht in London

„Ein deutscher Dachshund! Er hat mit seinem Schwanz dem Zeppelin ein Zeichen gegeben!"

„Verdammter deutscher Spion!!"

„Feuer!!!"

In the first few months of the war, a sort of anti-German hysteria affected Britain. Targets included German traders who had long resided in Britain, many of whose shops were smashed; imagined spies; and even dachshunds. These delightful little dogs were so persecuted that it became necessary to restart the breed in Britain from German stock after the war.

This German cartoon is entitled 'The spy-terror in London'. In the first frame, an urchin points to 'a German dachshund' – declaring that he had signalled to a Zeppelin airship with his tail. The crowd execrates the 'damned German spy' as he is led away by the police. In the final frame, the unfortunate animal is executed by a firing squad.

3

New ways of waging war

During the autumn of 1914, the war sank into deadlock on both eastern and western fronts, enormously costly both in men and in money. Neither side was prepared for that kind of war. Both therefore began to try various ways of breaking the deadlock.

The deadlock might be broken by 'traditional' methods: by developing new diplomatic and political initiatives, or new military strategies. Several such approaches were developed, and will be considered in the next chapter. The other possible way of breaking the deadlock, which will be considered in this chapter, was the development of new weapons and new techniques of warfare. Those techniques sometimes required high levels of technological skill. As a result, the two most technologically advanced states, Germany and Britain, tended to take the lead on their respective sides.

The first new technique turned on an extension of the traditional device of naval blockade. At the outbreak of war, Britain had considerably more naval vessels than Germany. Neither navy had any desire to risk attrition comparable with what the various armies were experiencing, nor a series of huge naval engagements. In practice, the British navy largely controlled the waters round Britain, while the main complement of the German navy remained in safe harbour, although there were sorties and attacks in both directions. Each side sought to do whatever was possible to prevent supplies, whether of military material or of civilian requirements such as food, from reaching the other.

Because of their relative strengths and weaknesses on the open sea, the British were able to employ surface vessels to hold up merchant ships which were carrying supplies to the enemy, while the Germans were more reliant on submarines and use of the torpedo. Both sides necessarily angered neutrals by these activities, and both were anxious to avert driving those neutrals to support the other side.

Sometimes civilian populations were more directly targeted. In December 1914, German battle-cruisers ventured across the North Sea and bombarded towns on the east coast of England. In January 1915 Zeppelin airships began to bomb English towns. Most of these raids inflicted substantial civilian casualties, but they were not on a scale to spread the general terror which had been intended. In time, the British replied more or less in kind. It would seem that the various raids were counter-productive, in that the damage inflicted was relatively slight, while public opinion in the victim countries was not yet familiar with the idea of civilians being used as direct targets of war, and was deeply shocked by the whole business.

Just as these new techniques of warfare against civilians added to the horrors of war, but gave little advantage to the perpetrators, so also was the major new development targeted against fighting men a doubtful asset. In the course of 1915 chlorine gas was used by the Germans, first on the eastern front and then on the western front. Later in the year, the Allies replied with the same material. A great many people suffered much pain, some of them for many years after the war, but it would be difficult to point to any important strategic advantage which any belligerent state received from its use.

Cartoon 3.1 Il n'y a plus ... *Le Charivari*, Paris, 14.iii.1915

— Il n'y a plus que moi qui fait de bonnes affaires.

In this French cartoon of March 1915, Death declares that he is now the only one who is doing well. Neither side was making perceptible progress in any theatre of war, but casualty lists were mounting rapidly as futile attacks continued.

In these circumstances, both sides attempted to develop new techniques of warfare which might affect the military situation.

Cartoon 3.2 Engeland houdt veel ... *De Amsterdammer*, Amsterdam, 22.xi.1914

ENGELAND HOUDT VEEL VAN DE NEUTRALEN, MAAR HET H Ó U D T OOK VEEL VAN DE NEUTRALEN!

This Dutch cartoon expresses a neutral's view of the war. In the latter part of 1914 the British commenced a general blockade of Germany. This involved intercepting neutral vessels and preventing them from delivering cargoes. The blockade applied not only to war material but also to food and other goods. The object was evidently to evidently to encourage a German collapse through starvation and other civilian privations.

The cartoon turns on a pun on the Dutch phrase 'houden van', which can mean either to love or to keep. The text suggests that Britain has great love for the neutrals, but keeps a lot of things belonging to neutrals. John Bull is hauling in neutral vessels with his trident, Britannia is examining them closely, and setting them down on the shore beside her.

Cartoon 3.3 His latest Battue. *Westminster Gazette*, London, 17.v.1915

HIS LATEST BATTUE.

The Kaiser is very fond of being photographed after a battue in his fantastic Imperial hunting costume, designed by himself.

Germany did not have enough surface naval vessels to reply in kind to the British blockade methods considered in the previous cartoon. Her most powerful blockade weapon was the submarine, which was very difficult to observe and control – even by an enemy which had mastery of the open seas. It was impossible for a submarine to stop and search merchant vessels and prevent them reaching an enemy port. All that the submarine could do was to sink the vessel. If it did so, there was often little or no prospect of rescuing survivors. In February 1915 Germany announced her intention of sinking vessels which violated her own blockade rules.

In May 1915 a German submarine sank the liner *Lusitania*, travelling to Britain from the United States. Well over a thousand people died, including 124 Americans. This enormous loss of life, overwhelmingly of civilian passengers, greatly shocked world opinion, particularly in the United States. America remained neutral for a long time to come; but there was no doubt that United States sympathy, already strongly favouring the Allies, was thereafter overwhelmingly pro-Allied.

In this cartoon, Wilhelm II and Admiral von Tirpitz, Head of the German Naval Staff, survey the civilian victims, many of whom are evidently children. In this period, the Kaiser and von Tirpitz attracted particular execration in Britain: far more than (for example) political figures such as the German Chancellor, von Bethmann Hollweg, or military figures like von Hindenburg.

Cartoon 3.4 The Zeppelin Raid on Ipswich. *New York Herald*, New York, 1.v.1915

THE ZEPPELIN RAID ON IPSWICH.

INCENDIARY BOMB

MISSED ANOTHER BABY.

In December 1914, German naval vessels made a few attacks on British coastal towns. In the following month, Zeppelin airships began to bomb urban targets, and these attacks were continued for a long time to come.

This American cartoon comments bitterly on these Zeppelin bombing raids. The tone of the cartoon suggests that these raids were not only causing great anger in Britain, but were also having a profoundly adverse effect on neutral opinion.

Cartoon 3.5 Feindliche Anertennung. *Fliegende Blätter,* Munich, 28.v.1915

---❦- Feindliche Anerkennung. -❦---

(Vor Ypern.) „Auch in der Chemie scheinen uns die Deutschen über zu sein."

This insensitive German cartoon of May 1915, 'Enemy Appreciation', refers to the first use of poison gas on the Western Front, at the battle of Ypres. The British soldiers going into battle admit that 'in chemistry too the Germans are ahead of us'. In fact there was nothing particularly advanced in the chemistry of the first poison gas, which was chlorine – a substance easily produced in the laboratory, whose preparation had long been attempted by students at quite an elementary stage of their studies.

The soldiers do not all wear the same uniform, but some are evidently kilted Scots. German cartoons of the time often portray Britons wearing kilts – sometimes with incongruously English garments on other parts of their bodies.

Later in the year the Allies also used poison gas. Neither side appears to have derived much advantage from its use, for a variety of reasons – including the risk that a change of wind would return the gas to the side which had sent it.

4

Mediterranean dramas, 1915

In the early part of 1915, Russian troops were under considerable pressure from the Turks in the vicinity of the Caucasus. Russia therefore urged the western Allies to force a way into the Black Sea, which would enable them to stage a relieving operation. Perhaps even at this stage of the war the British and French were beginning to wonder whether Russia might conclude a separate peace with Germany if she did not receive adequate assistance from the West.

Here was the genesis of the Dardanelles episode. The Allies sought to establish forces along the Bosporus and to capture the Ottoman capital, Constantinople. There was some reason for hoping that the Ottoman Empire was already so rotten that it would collapse completely if it were confronted with substantial forces from major Allied Powers. Had not the little Balkan countries nearly succeeded in driving the Turks from Europe as recently as 1912?

The Dardanelles expedition was a combined military and naval operation. Any prospect of a fairly easy Allied success depended on the different forces involved working closely together. That cooperation did not take place. A naval attack in February resulted in heavy losses. In April troops landed, but by the following month powerful voices were being raised for discontinuing the whole operation. This led to a considerable political crisis in Britain, and formation of the first Coalition government. The Dardanelles operation, however, continued until January 1916, when the last troops were evacuated. As on the great land fronts, vast numbers of casualties were incurred for few or no results.

The first half of 1915 was also marked by the entry of Italy into the war. The old Triple Alliance had not required Italy to fight on the side of the Central Powers, and at the start Italy was neutral. Italy had territorial aspirations both against France and against Austria-Hungary, and she might hope to satisfy one set of aspirations if she entered the war on the side which happened to win.

In the early spring of 1915, there was some bidding for Italian support – or at least benevolent neutrality – from both sides. In the end, the Allies were successful, and in April the secret Treaty of London was negotiated. As a result, Italy entered the war against Austria-Hungary in the following month. The new Italian front, however, was no more mobile than the others. Initial Italian advances were soon held up, and trench warfare followed.

So stood the war about the middle of 1915. An important new belligerent had entered the contest, new techniques had been devised for making war even nastier than before, new strategic plans had appeared, and political changes had been introduced. Yet nobody was any closer to victory, or any other kind of resolution of the war.

Cartoon 4.1 Making the feathers fly. *New Zealand Herald,* Auckland, 8.v.1915

MAKING THE FEATHERS FLY.

News was received in New Zealand on April 29 that New Zealand troops were included in the allied forces attacking the Turkish positions in the Dardanelles. Later cable messages state that they had been constantly in touch with the enemy for several days, and were pushing on with "the utmost boldness" and "with fine spirit and determination."

—AUCKLAND WEEKLY NEWS.

In this Dominion cartoon, the New Zealand kiwi impales three turkeys.

In April 1915 Allied troops, many of them from Australia and New Zealand ('ANZACS'), landed at the Dardanelles, and managed to secure a bridgehead. Initially the Australians and New Zealanders took great pride in the operation, but it soon proved to be a great deal less successful than this optimistic cartoon suggested.

Carton 4.2 Das deutsche Volksleid im Weltkriege.
Kladderadatsch, Berlin, 7.xi.1915

Das deutsche Volkslied im Weltkriege

General Hamilton ist von den
Dardanellen abberufen worden

Abschied von den Dardanellen: „Nun leb' wohl, du kleine Gasse!"

The Allied naval and military expedition to the Dardanelles seemed at
one point to have a substantial chance of radically altering the course of
the war. In the end it proved a disastrous failure.

   This German cartoon commemorates the final collapse of the Dardanelles
expedition at the turn of 1915–16. General Sir Ian Hamilton, the British
officer who had been in charge of the expedition, bids a tearful farewell to
the Dardanelles, over which the Turkish flag still flies triumphantly.

Cartoon 4.3 High explosive shells. *The Bystander*, London, 2.vi.1915

HIGH EXPLOSIVE SHELLS
The New Cabinet arrives in the Treasury Trench

In May 1915, failure of the Dardanelles operation to deliver early and positive results to the Allies produced intense criticism of the British government's handling of the war. In the ordinary course of events, a General Election would have been due later in the year, but all parties were anxious to avoid a serious political showdown in the middle of the war. In the end, the matter was temporarily resolved by formation of the first Coalition government.

This British cartoon commemorates the Coalition. Reading from left to right, the front row of the marchers is made up of the Marquess of Crewe (Liberal; Lord President of Council), A. J. Balfour (Unionist; Admiralty) and H. H. Asquith (Liberal; Prime Minister). In the second row are D. Lloyd George (Liberal; Minister of Munitions), Sir Edward Carson (Unionist; Attorney–General) and A. Bonar Law (Unionist; Colonial Office). In the third row are Austen Chamberlain (Unionist; India Office) and Arthur Henderson (Labour; Education). The figure on the extreme right is Winston Churchill (Liberal; Duchy of Lancaster). The identity of the man beside him is not clear. Several members of the Cabinet are not shown.

The Coalition government was probably appointed more for political than for military reasons. It was difficult to see that the newcomers were likely to bring any significant qualities as war leaders which were not present in the old government.

Cartoon 4.4 Vicarious generosity. *Punch*, London, 24.iv.1915

VICARIOUS GENEROSITY.

KAISER. "SHOULD YOU WANT SOME MORE FEATHERS, I KNOW A TWO-HEADED EAGLE."

Italy was neutral at the beginning of the war. In the spring of 1915, both sides were concerned, if possible, to bring her into the war as a fighting ally and, at worst, to ensure her continuing neutrality. Neither side considered that any very exalted ideas would influence Italy's decision.

In this *Punch* cartoon, 'Vicarious generosity', the German Emperor attempts to attract Italy to his side. He hints strongly that he 'knows a two-headed eagle' who might provide 'some more feathers' – i.e., that he can exert influence on Austria–Hungary to persuade her to cede some territory which Italy covets. The eagle looks less than happy about the matter which is being discussed. The Italian shows interest in the offer.

Eventually Italy was persuaded to enter the war – but on the Allied side – by the secret Treaty of London, which promised her considerable slices of Austro–Hungarian territory in exchange. In May 1915 Italy declared war on Austria–Hungary, although some time elapsed before she also declared war on Germany.

Cartoon 4.5 Il momento politico. *Avanti,*
Milan, 17.v.1915

Il momento politico

The Italian socialist periodical *Avanti* was opposed to the idea that the country should enter the war. This cartoon appeared a few days before Italy declared war on Austria–Hungary. King Victor Emmanuel III pushes blindfolded Italy towards the end of what looks like the blade of a knife. This is cutting her feet, and blood is pouring from the wounds. The King, who seems to be wearing tough military boots, is uninjured. If the progress continues, Italy will eventually fall on to the pointed weapons – perhaps bayonets – which are set underneath. The message seems to be that matters are already bad, and are likely to get worse.

Cartoon 4.6 Gleich und gleich ... *Der Brummer*, Berlin, No. 60, 1915

Gleich und gleich gesellt sich gern.

Musolino hat seine Entlassung beantragt, um bei der glorreichen Armee kämpfen zu können.

MUSOLINO   D'ANNUNZIO

Ein Herzensbund ist tief gegründet, wenn sich der Lump zum Lumpen findet.

This German cartoon (whose caption like the caption of 2.2, means, roughly, 'Birds of a feather flock together') is remarkable as a very early international portrayal of Benito Mussolini. At that time he wore a beard, and he was still not sufficiently well known for the cartoonist to get the spelling of the future dictator's name right.

The man on the right of the picture is the highly 'respectable' and charismatic Italian poet and novelist, Gabriele d'Annunzio, whose advocacy of Italy's entry to the war may have played a substantial part in the eventual decision. D'Annunzio appears frequently in German cartoons of the period.

Mussolini was a man of much humbler background, who had been editor of the socialist *Avanti*, but who disagreed with that periodical's anti-war views, and later founded his own publication *Il Popolo d'Italia*. Evidently his portrayal here as a sort of brigand is a reflection on his origins and early opinions. However, the two men have now come together in support of the war; hence the cartoonist sees them as 'equals'.

5

Changing patterns

As has been seen, the war developed in a manner completely different from the anticipation of political or military leaders in any country. Unlike most previous wars, in which only small minorities had been actively engaged, the Great War rapidly became a 'war of peoples', which affected the lives and outlooks of nearly everybody in the belligerent countries. Large changes of attitude took place – some of them closely related to the war itself, others much more indirectly related.

The most obvious and direct involvement of people in the war was through recruitment. At the outbreak of war, most European countries already had military conscription, and the business of recruitment was essentially one of calling up more and more classes of trained reservists, plus other men who had just reached military age. This process inevitably caused all kinds of economic dislocation; but the immediate business was relatively straightforward, and did not cause too many political difficulties.

In Britain, by contrast, there was no tradition of conscription – essentially because Britain's main defence had always been by sea, and naval defence was far less labour-intensive than land defence. Adequate supplies of sailors, and of soldiers too, could be secured by voluntary enlistment. The process by which Britain edged towards conscription was a painful and gradual one which will be considered in the light of cartoons.

There were parallel problems with armaments. Everyone had planned for a war of movement; nobody had anticipated prolonged trench warfare. Because military leaders soon decided that the best way of attempting to dislodge entrenched enemies was by using ballistic missiles, there was a general shells crisis in 1915. The shells question played a large part, along with the Dardanelles question, in producing the British Coalition government of 1915.

The disappearance of men into armies, and the need both for shells and for the guns to fire them, produced another kind of crisis. Labour became desperately short. This led to growing recruitment of women into what before 1914 most people had regarded as 'men's work'. This in turn would soon give impetus to a demand by women for something much closer to social and political equality with men: a matter which will be considered later.

The various warlike operations cost enormous sums of money – vastly more than taxpayers in any country were accustomed to pay. Taxes, inevitably, were increased, but there was also a growing disposition for governments to borrow through war loans and other means. In all probability, the various politicians reached the private and unannounced conclusion that, in the event of victory, they would be able to extract much of the cost of war from the defeated enemy. Few people on either side bothered much about what would happen in case of defeat.

At quite an early stage of the war, there were signs of new, emerging, nationalisms. As had already been seen, some of the British Dominions were soon engaged in warfare of one kind or another. Neither the Dominion cartoons nor those from Britain itself leave much doubt that an intense national pride was developing there. In the early part of the war, most of this new national pride was generally welcomed in the Allied countries, but it had long-term implications which might have been less welcome.

In other cases the new nationalisms which were generated by war were less pleasing to the side on which they appeared; indeed, in some cases they were highly embarrassing to both sides. Much of the fighting on the Eastern Front took place in land which had once been Poland, and Poles could hardly be expected to fight each other with much enthusiasm in the service of countries which, in the past, had divided Poland between them. These nationalisms were only beginning to emerge in 1915, but before the war was over they would play a major part in tearing apart four great empires.

Apart from the dissident nationalities, and a few individuals who for one reason or another objected to war as such, most people in the belligerent countries soon made a more or less complete identification with the cause of their national governments. This identification not only made them willing to support the waging of war, at whatever cost, but it also made them identify all individuals in foreign countries with the governments which presided over those countries.

Stories – some true, some false, some distorted – were rapidly circulated in all countries, recording acts of bravery performed by their own compatriots, or by citizens of Allied countries. So also were stories circulated of atrocities committed by people belonging to enemy countries. Within a very short time, most people failed to distinguish between praiseworthy or blameworthy individuals and the general population of the country to which those individuals belonged. This kind of identification occurred in most, and perhaps in all, countries.

In these circumstances, the war rapidly acquired a momentum of its own, unrelated to any war aims which the various governments may have entertained at the beginning. No governments, not even the most despotic governments, really had much control over that phenomenon. Most of them had been able to lead their peoples into war without much difficulty; by 1915, none of them could have made peace even if they had sought to do so.

Cartoon 5.1 Le malade et la conscription anglaise. *Le Journal*, Paris, 16.i.1916

LE MALADE ET LA CONSCRIPTION ANGLAISE

— *Cette fois je suis kapout ! !...*

(Dessin de RICARDO FLORES.)

At the turn of 1915–16 the British government finally decided to intro-
duce military conscription. At first this only applied to unmarried men,
but later in 1916 married men were conscripted as well.

This French cartoon suggests that the 'sick' Kaiser, reading the news
about British conscription, would decide that 'this time I am kaput'. If
the war were to be decided by the relative capacity of the two sides to
wear each other down by attrition, there was some force in that view.
Conscription, however, was not welcomed by all military men, for some
considered that the efficiency of a volunteer force would be reduced by
drafting and training unwilling conscripts.

Cartoon 5.2 A cheerful giver. *Punch,* London, 12.v.1915

A CHEERFUL GIVER.

In Britain, as in all other belligerent countries, the war produced an enormous increase in taxation and state spending. This rather optimistic cartoon of May 1915 commemorates the great departure from traditional public finance which had already developed by that date.

Figures must, of course, be understood in the money values of the time. By all tests, however, the expenditure bore no comparison with anything experienced before that date. The previous year's budget had planned for expenditure well under a fifth of that proposed for 1915–16.

The picture of John Bull shouldering the burden rather suggests that he was sustaining it all through increased taxation, That, however, was very far from the truth. Taxes were, of course, increased, but it was also necessary to raise huge sums by loans, by sale of assets, and by other financial expedients. Britain's world economic position was profoundly and permanently weakened.

Cartoon 5.3 Die Anspannung der Bank von England.
Kladderadatsch, Berlin, 27.vi.1915

Die Anspannung der Bank von England

Wie lange wird fie es noch aushalten?

'The strain on the Bank of England' is a German view of the great increase in British expenditure, and turns on the ambiguity of the word 'Bank', which in German preserves its old meaning of 'bench' as well as its derived meaning as a repository for money.

   In this cartoon, loans for Britain's various allies are imposing a great strain on the bench, and the cartoonist wonders how long it will continue to bear the load. There can be little doubt that British financial support was of major importance in enabling existing Allies to continue fighting, and in persuading neutrals to come over to support the Allies.

Cartoon 5.4 Sankt Georg . . . *Kladderadatsch,*
Berlin, 18.iv.1914

Kladderadatsch. Berlin, 18 April 1915

Sankt Georg von England, der Drachentöter

In the late nineteenth and early twentieth centuries, the British had a bad
reputation for drunkenness, particularly the abuse of spirits, which was
sometimes commemorated in French as well as German cartoons. In the
early part of the war, drunkenness increased considerably in Britain, and it
was widely thought that this had a seriously adverse effect on the war effort.
Various legislative and taxation devices were used to control this phenomenon, but particular attention was given to the 'King's Pledge'. George V
undertook to abstain from alcohol himself for the duration of the war, and
to exclude it from his household, as an example to his subjects.

The 'King's Pledge' is commemorated in this rather sympathetic German
cartoon. King George is drawn in the character of his saintly namesake,
slaying the dragon Drink. Curiously, the image of the King fighting the
dragon 'War Drink Problem' was also used on the Allied side, in a *London
Opinion* cartoon of the previous day. Evidently each cartoonist conceived
the idea independently, and neither was copying from the other.

41

Cartoon 5.5 Jack Canuck robs the eagle's nest.
Toronto World, Toronto, 6.v.1915

In all British Dominions, military exploits of the First World War helped to foster a sense of nationhood. Canadians played a large part on the Western Front. In this Canadian cartoon, Jack Canuck – the Canadian equivalent of John Bull or Uncle Sam – 'robs the eagle's nest' by seizing the egg Langemarck from the crag Ypres, to the distress of the German eagle. Jack wears on his back the Roll of Honour, commemorating the great bravery of Canadians on this occasion, which attracted much admiration in Allied circles.

At the second Battle of Ypres, in April and May 1915, Canadian troops played a major part in holding back a serious German attack, at which poison gas was used. In fact, the town of Langemarck was lost by the Allies later in the battle, and was not regained until two years later. Ypres, however, was saved.

Cartoon 5.6 The gentle German. From Edmund J. Sullivan: *The Kaiser's Garden*, William Heinemann, London, 1915

This cartoon of 1915 casts light on a weapon of growing importance, which was extensively used by both sides: hate propaganda.

The winged figure impaled on the German bayonet in this British cartoon is clearly allegorical, and is possibly meant to be Love. Nevertheless, the reader is being invited to visualise actual German soldiers impaling actual human infants on bayonets.

No Briton was likely to encounter a German impaling a child, but the soldier going into battle was encouraged to see this evil figure in the enemy soldier whom he was trying to kill, and the man who had not joined the army was encouraged to do so in order to take part in the destruction of such monsters.

It would be wrong to think of the authors of 'hate cartoons' as cynical exploiters of public gullibility. Probably most of them sincerely believed in the essential truth of the message they were imparting.

6

War in the East, 1915

The second half of 1915 saw little dramatic change in the character of the war, except in the area bordering on the eastern Mediterranean. The expedition to Gallipoli finally collapsed, but an alternative Allied strategy appeared in the southern Balkans. This new strategy was not so much concerned with forcing the Bosporus (although it could have had some effect in that direction), but rather with assisting Serbia. In the course of 1915, Serbia and Montenegro came under increasing military pressure from Germany and Austria–Hungary, and so the western Allies sought to render assistance through operations from Salonika (Thessaloniki) in Greece, which communicated through the Vardar valley with Serbia.

The position was anomalous in several ways. Greece was neutral, but the King, Constantine I/XII (the remarkable difference of Royal numbering depends on whether or not the eleven Byzantine emperors of that name are included in the succession), was a close relative of the Kaiser, while the Prime Minister, Eleftherios Venizelos, favoured the Allies. The Greek government more or less connived at Allied landings at Salonika, which commenced in October 1915. Meanwhile a long and complex series of political intrigues was set in motion, which would outlast the war itself.

The Allied operations through Greece more or less coincided with activities equally thick with intrigue, but to the opposite effect, in Bulgaria. The legacy of Bulgarian resentment from the Second Balkan War of 1913 made it fairly easy for the Central Powers to persuade King Ferdinand to commence operations against Serbia, with the object of securing territorial gains at Serbia's expense.

The effect of the Bulgarian westward thrust was to block the Allied move northwards up the Vardar valley. The foothold at Salonika, however, was retained. This had little military value in the circumstances, and tied up many troops until the end of the war. The unfortunate Serbs and Montenegrins were defeated, but a few remnants of their forces were able to take refuge on the Greek island of Corfu.

The shadowy independence of Egypt had been swept aside early in the war, and the country declared a British protectorate. By the end of 1915, the British position in Egypt was being sapped from two sides. Libyan tribesmen attacked the Italians who had recently colonised their country, and also the British across the Egyptian frontier, while Turks under German command prepared a force east of Sinai.

In other areas on the Ottoman fringe, important developments took place in the second half of 1915. In the early part of the war. British troops from India had pushed into what is now known as Iraq, but was then usually called Mesopotamia, and was still an Ottoman province. At first the venture was attended with some success but in late 1915 the British were pushed back.

Grimmer events still occurred in eastern Anatolia. Armenians extended over parts of Turkey, Russia and Persia. In the Ottoman Empire there were few places where they constituted a majority, but many in which they formed a substantial minority. After the long tally of Turkish atrocities in the 1890s and the early twentieth century, no Armenians could have failed to desire an Ottoman defeat. In the autumn of 1915 this profound alienation led to a series of Turkish massacres of Armenians on a far greater scale than before – an event which seems to anticipate the holocaust of Jews in the 1940s. Enormous numbers of Armenians perished: a conservative figure is 600,000 but the total may well have been far greater than that.

Cartoon 6.1 The call of the Tsar. *Punch*, London, 15.ix.1915

THE CALL OF THE TSAR.

"WHO FOLLOWS ME FOR HOLY RUSSIA'S SAKE?"

From the spring of 1915 onwards, Russian troops on the Eastern Front were increasingly hard-pressed by the Central Powers. Early in September, the Tsar took personal overall command of the Russian army, displacing his uncle the Grand Duke Nicholas. The event is commemorated in this British cartoon.

Like the formation of the British Coalition government in May of the same year, this action must be seen as of political rather than military significance. It is difficult to see what exceptional personal qualities the Tsar could bring to the direction of the war. It was, however, a sign of the growing desperation of the Russian government.

Cartoon 6.2 Vystupil. *Novoe Vremya,* Petrograd, 10/23.x.1915

ВЫСТУПИЛИ.

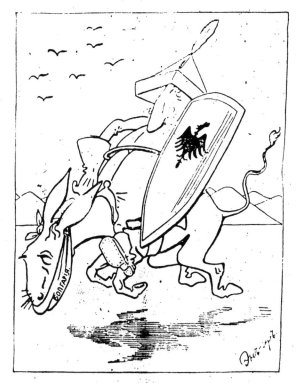

Балканскій рыцарь «не безъ страха и упрека».

Early in October 1915, Bulgaria entered the war on the side of the Central Powers, aiming to secure Serbian territory.

In this Russian cartoon 'Coming out', King Ferdinand of Bulgaria emerges as the 'Balkan key factor, "not without fear and reproach" '. The steed Bulgaria on which he is mounted is gagged. The cartoonist evidently believed that the Bulgarian people, if permitted to speak for themselves, would have repudiated the King's action.

Cartoon 6.3 Our friend the butcher. *Westminster Gazette,* London, 19.x.1915

OUR FRIEND THE BUTCHER.

KAISER : *Our friend the Butcher ! (Aside.) It's all right, Ferdinand-- it's only* ARMENIAN BLOOD *this time !*

The decision of Bulgaria to enter the war on the same side as Turkey was astonishing to those recalling the 'Bulgarian horrors' of the 1870s, and even the First Balkan War of 1912. The paradox was even more poignant, for at the same moment a new series of Ottoman atrocities was taking place, on an even greater scale, against the Armenians.

The cartoonist was a Liberal who was old enough to remember Gladstone's campaigns against both the 'Bulgarian horrors', and the earlier spates of Armenian atrocities. The Kaiser attempts to reassure King Ferdinand of Bulgaria, and encourages him to grasp the bloodstained hand of Sultan Mohammed V.

The scale of the renewed Armenian atrocities completely dwarfed anything which had happened in modern times down to that date, and provided a baleful precedent for later acts of genocide. Although the existence of the atrocities was well known to contemporaries, surprisingly little attention was given to them by cartoonists or other propagandists.

Cartoon 6.4 The persuading of Tino. *Punch*, London, 24.xi.1915

THE PERSUADING OF TINO.

This British cartoon is set in a classical style, imitating the design of an Attic vase. It considers the difficult position of King Constantine ('Tino') of Greece. Despite the Allied landings at Salonika, his country was still neutral.

Brett (Britain) and Gall (France) attempt to pull the King one way, while Kais(er), with the approval of Ferdi(nand) pulls in the other direction. The inscription at the top, 'Perdix did (it)' emulates the potter's signature sometimes applied to these vases. 'Perdix', in Classical Greek (as also in Latin), means 'partridge', which identifies the artist as Sir Bernard Partridge, who drew a number of the *Punch* cartoons here illustrated.

Cartoon 6.5 The new Triple Alliance. *New York Tribune*, New York, copied in Boardman Robinson: *Cartoons of the War*, J.M. Dent & Sons, London, 1915

An important question for diplomats and strategists in all countries was to decide who was the principal enemy against whom the main attack should be aimed.

'The new Triple Alliance' is an American cartoon. In the Alliance (i.e., the Central Powers), only the German Emperor looks strong and healthy; the Austrian is badly wounded and in a wheelchair, while the Turk looks feeble. Whether this view would have been universally endorsed in Allied circles is uncertain. The Gallipoli expedition showed that the Turks were a good deal stronger than many had thought. There can be little doubt however that most people in Britain and France regarded Germany as the most important, and also as the strongest, enemy thoughout the war.

Cartoon 6.6 Keine Ahnung von Theorie! *Der Brummer,* Berlin, No. 33, 1915

Keine Ahnung von Theorie!

„Hurra, ein Stoss frische Zeitungen aus Deutschland!

Aha, Russland ist der Hauptfeind! geben wir ihm also eins!

Hm! Das scheint mir ja ein schöner Missgriff gewesen zu sein. Der Hauptfeind ist ja England. Na, denn da, du Viech!

Sakra! Sakra! Da steht klipp und klar, dass es Russland ist. Na, denn man feste druff!

Himmelkreuzbombenelement — es ist doch England!

Ach Gott, ach Gott! Was wird man bloss zu Hause sagen — jetzt sind sie alle beide hin!"

51

In Germany, by contrast, there was considerable doubt in the course of 1915 as to who was the principal enemy, as this cartoon shows. The soldier reads different German newspapers, some suggesting that Russia was the principal enemy and others suggesting that it was Britain. Inspired by their various views, he assaults both enemies with equal enthusiasm and success, but finally wonders what the people at home will say when he has defeated both of them. The representative of Britain (which the cartoonist insists on calling 'England') wears Scottish, not English, dress – perhaps because this was considered more distinctive.

Although far more Germans were currently being killed by Frenchmen than by Britons, it is noteworthy that none of the newspapers seemed to consider that France had any claim to be the principal enemy.

7

War for its own sake

In the first half of 1916 the war became more and more pointless for both sides. The original war aims of the Great Powers had either been attained, or else could only be attained at a cost quite incommensurate with any possible benefit.

Various strategies, diplomatic and military, had been tried by both sides in order to win a swift victory. The German Schieffen Plan had failed in its primary purpose, and had involved Britain as an extra enemy. The Allied Dardanelles expedition had been an unqualified disaster, and the new Salonika expedition tied down great number of troops to little avail. Germany had won no decisive advantage from involving Turkey and Bulgaria in the war on her side, nor had the Allies won any decisive advantage from involving Italy.

There was no good reason for thinking that anybody would come up with any new way of producing a swift victory at low cost to themseleves. Conscript armies were pitted against each other in vast numbers in East and West alike. At Verdun and on the Somme vast numbers of soldiers perished on both sides, in appalling conditions, for no significant territorial gain. On the Eastern Front it was not very different.

At sea the struggle seemed as bleak and pointless as it was on land, although fortunately the admirals were not as keen on attrition as were the generals. Despite the extraordinary Battle of Jutland, both sides gave principal attention to securing an economic stranglehold on the enemy, rather than through naval warfare of the tradtional kind. The weapon was blockade, which each side sought to apply by the methods available: the British using surface ships in order to starve Germany, the Germans using submarines to sink ships bringing merchandise to British shores. The paradox was that the more effective these measures became the more likely it was that important countries which were still neutral, most particularly the United States, would be driven into war on the opposite side.

Everybody could see that the drain of men and of wealth had already been enormous, and would become much greater if the war continued: far greater than any compensation which they could realistically hope to extract from a defeated enemy. Bolshevism had not yet appeared as a great international force; but the various political and military leaders must have perceived dimly that defeat would bring their regimes to ruin, and that even victory would not return them to the internal security they had known before the war. No inspiring war aims had been invented, which might somehow persuade the ordinary people that the suffering and sacrifice were justified for the hope of some future gain.

Cartoon 7.1 Verdun. *San Francisco Chronicle*, 2.iii.1916

❖ ❖ ❖ ❖ VERDUN ❖ ❖ ❖ ❖

The struggle for Verdun, which lasted through most of 1916, was one of the most horrific battles of attrition ever fought. In the end, two-thirds of a million men were killed, approximately half on each side.

This American cartoon requires no words. Even Death and Mars are horrified at the carnage.

Cartoon 7.2 Heimgeschickt. *Fliegende Blätter*, Munich, 30.vi.1916

31 Mai   HEIMGESCHICKT.   1916.

This cartoon is a reminder that the full results of a battle are sometimes not clear until long after the fighting is over. It is one of a number of German cartoons gloating over the results of the Battle of Jutland in May 1916.

Jutland was the most important naval engagement of the war, and appears generally to have been regarded at the time as an important, though not decisive, German victory over their British opponents. Certainly more British vessels than German were sunk, and British cartoons of the time do not seem to suggest anything very different from the German view.

It now seems clear that Jutland was, in truth, a very important triumph for the British, for thereafter the German High Seas Fleet did not venture in force into open water. If that Fleet had been able to do so, the upshot of the war might have been very different from what it was.

Cartoon 7.3 Na Kavkaze. *Novoe Vremya,* Petrograd, 2/15.iv.1916

НА КАВКАЗѢ.

— Гдѣ это тебя такъ угоравдило?
— Въ Эрзерумѣ—русскимъ попался!

Although most of the battles of early 1916 were indecisive and enormously costly, the Russians were faring rather well in their campaigns on the Turkish frontier.

In this Russian cartoon, 'In the Caucasus', the Kaiser encounters an injured Turk, and asks him where he had been wounded. He replies that it was at Erzerum, at the hands of the Russians. Erzerum was in the part of eastern Anatolia where Armenians had once been numerous, but where they had recently been massacred.

Cartoon 7.4 You're next, John. *Chicago Daily Tribune,*
Chicago, 10.ii.1916

This American cartoon comments on the difficult relations between the
United States – by far the most important of the remaining neutrals –
and belligerents on both sides.

Uncle Sam has just interviewed the German, to whom he had
complained bitterly over the *Lusitania* case of the previous year.
Remonstrations on the subject were still continuing, and these were playing
an important part in domestic American politics as well as international
affairs. The German's expression is not visible, but he does not seem
pleased. John Bull, however, is due for the next interview and will clearly
also receive sharp criticism for his blockade policy.

Both Britain and Germany were conscious of the need to avoid angering
the United States too much. The *Lusitania* incident, and the fury which
it roused in the United States, played an important part in compelling
Germany to play down her submarine campaign for the time being. Britain
also perceived the need to be wary in her blockade policy.

Cartoon 7.5 Nouvelle Génération. *Le Canard Enchaîné,* Paris, 29.xi.1916

NOUVELLE GÉNÉRATION

— Et toi, mon petit, qu'est-ce que tu feras quand tu auras vingt ans ?
— Je mourrai pour la patrie, m'sieur !

This French cartoon comments bleakly on the apparently endless character of the war. The elderly man asks the boy what he proposes to do when he is twenty. The reply: 'I shall die for the country, sir!' In the background are the next two waves of cannon fodder: the little boy with a hoop, and the baby in a perambulator.

It is rather surprising that the authorities allowed such a cartoon to be published at all, for its message was 'defeatist'. The French army was on the verge of mutiny.

8

The smaller nations, 1916

In the course of 1916, considerable attention was given by both sides to ways in which small nations might be rallied to their respective causes. Perhaps small neutral countries might be brought into the war; perhaps people belonging to 'minority' nationalities living under enemy rule might be induced to revolt against those rulers.

The Allies contrived, without too much difficulty, to bring two new belligerents into the war: Romania and Portugal. In the first case, the main attraction appears to have been possible territorial gains. Romania had designs on the Austro–Hungarian provinces of Transylvania and Bukovina, and perhaps on Bulgarian parts of the Dobruja. In the case of Portugal, too, territorial aspirations may have played some part, for she had African possessions on each side of the continent which were contiguous with pre-war German colonies, and may have seen some point in goading Germany to declare war. The immediate cause, however, was different. Both new recruits were to prove very dubious assets.

The most spectacular example of the use of subversion in small subject nations to embarrass major enemies occurred in Ireland, although the pattern which events took in that country was quite different from the original intentions of Germany. In the early part of the war, the Germans made some effort to recruit supporters among Irish prisoners-of-war. Very few responded. Later, the prospect of an insurrection in Ireland itself appeared on the scene. At the last minute the Germans sought to call it off. The insurrection took place all the same, and produced long-term consequences which can hardly have been anticipated by either side.

The Central Powers took more positive action to rally the Poles to their side. On the whole, Poles had been worse-treated by the Russians than by the Austrians and Prussians who had taken their own shares of Poland in the late eighteenth century. Furthermore, the Russian slice of Poland was the largest of the three, and included that part of former Poland which was ethnically most purely Polish. Towards the end of 1916, the Central Powers announced their intention to establish a kingdom of Poland within the parts of Russian Poland occupied by their troops, and simultaneously Austria–Hungary promised autonomy for Galicia, which had been its own share of the former Polish state.

In 1916, the Allies also commenced serious internal subversion. Their immediate target was the Ottoman Empire. Most of the former Christian subjects of the Empire had either become independent within the previous century, or had been scattered or massacred. There remained, however, a large and important body of non-Turkish Moslems, of whom the Arabs were most numerous.

Cartoon 8.1 Ireland. *Simplicissimus*, Munich, 16.v.1916

„Diefe Waffe haft mir du geliefert, nicht Deutfchland!"

All significant Irish politicians, Nationalist and Unionist alike, supported the war. Yet popular enthusiasm for that war, as measured by voluntary recruitment to the services, was a good deal lower in some parts of Ireland than anywhere in Great Britain. When conscription was introduced in Britain early in 1916, it was not thought advisable to attempt to apply it to Ireland.

On Easter Monday 1916, a group of Irish extremists seized certain buildings in Dublin and proclaimed the 'Irish Republic'. At one time the Germans had had some interest in fomenting a rising of this kind, but they later decided that it was unwise to do so, and the rebellion was soon stamped out.

In this German cartoon, the Irishman assaults John Bull with a chain, declaring '*You* gave me this weapon (i.e., the chain of oppression), not Germany'.

Cartoon 8.2 Vengeance! *Irish World,* New York, 13.v.1916

PATRICK H. PEARSE
THOMAS J. CLARKE
THOMAS McDONAGH
JOSEPH PLUNKETT
EDWARD DALY
M. O'HANRAHAN
WILLIAM PEARSE
JOHN McBRIDE
CORNELIUS CULBERT
J. J. HEUSTON
EAMONN CEANNT
MICHAEL MALLON

ROLL OF IRISH HEROES

VENGEANCE!

This cartoon appeared in May 1916 in the *Irish World,* a profoundly anti-British New York periodical, aimed mainly at people of Irish descent in the United States.

In the aftermath of the Easter Week Rising, many of the ringleaders were first tried in secret, and then shot. This *Irish World* cartoon expresses deep anger at the executions.

While the rising itself had had little popular support, the executions transformed the victims into popular heroes. The reaction was not immediate (despite the suggestion to the contrary in the *Irish World*); but, as the war continued, Catholic Ireland became increasingly alienated from the Allied cause.

The events of Easter Week were profoundly embarrassing to the British in many places outside Ireland. They made it difficult to 'sell' the Allied case in countries like the United States where there were many people of Irish extraction, and sceptics were disposed to contrast British enthusiasm for small countries like Belgium and Serbia with their attitude to Ireland.

Cartoon 8.3 Die Neidischen. *Kladderadatsch,* Berlin, 17.xii.1916

Die Neidischen

„Nun seht mal den kleinen Polen! Bei den Mittelmächten gibt's zu Weihnachten Geschenke, bei uns nur -- Prügel!"

The Central Powers were also interested in the idea of subverting Polish subjects of the Russian Empire. Early in November 1916, it was announced that they proposed to create an autonomous Polish kingdom in the districts of Russian Poland which they occupied, while the Austrians simultaneously announced a scheme for giving autonomy to Galicia, or 'Austrian Poland'.

In the German cartoon, 'The Jealous Ones', the young Pole stands by the Christmas tree, carrying the White Eagle flag and trying on his new crown. In the background, the dispossessed kings of Serbia, Belgium, Montenegro and Romania, whose countries were largely occupied by troops of the Central Powers, contrast the little Pole's fate with their own. To him, they mutter, the Central Powers have given Christmas presents: to themselves, only a beating.

Cartoon 8.4 Not exactly ... *The Bystander,* London, 28.vi.1916

Not Exactly What They Had in Mind!

SULTAN MEHMET: " Yes, I see, Brother, we have raised a ' Holy War ' all right— b-b-b-but it's c-c-coming the wrong w-w-way !!! "

The Allies were as eager as the Central Powers to subvert potentially hostile subjects of enemy countries. In June 1916, disaffected Arab subjects of the Ottoman Empire, with encouragement from the Allies, seized Mecca – whose military importance was perhaps small, but whose emotional significance for Moslems was enormous.

In this cartoon, the Sultan and the Kaiser view these events with alarm. The cartoon suggests that the two monarchs had hoped to raise a jihad, or 'holy war', against the Allies – perhaps in Egypt, perhaps in Mesopotamia which the Allies were currently invading, perhaps even in the Moslem parts of India. Instead, the jihad was 'coming the wrong way'.

Cartoon 8.5 Rumänische Gäste. *Simplicissimus*, Munich, 24.x.1916

„Piffolo, nimm den Herrschaften die Kronen ab und führe sie auf die refervierten Zimmer!"

In 1916 Romania entered the war on the Allied side, evidently in the hope of making territorial gains at the expense of Austria-Hungary and Bulgaria.

After some early victories, the Romanians fared disastrously. 'Romanian guests' is a German comment on the situation, King Ferdinand of Romania (not to be confused with his namesake, the King of Bulgaria) and his wife arrive as refugees at the 'Hotel of the Fugitive Kings'. The French President, Raymond Poincaré, who is the proprietor, instructs his servant to remove the new guests' crowns and lead them to their room. Kings Nicholas of Montenegro, Peter of Serbia and Albert of the Belgians view the scene.

This cartoon is to a degree misleading, because the Romanian King was not actually driven from his country, although Bucharest was occupied by the Central Powers.

Cartoon 8.6 Muzey v Athenakh. *Novoe Vremya,* Petrograd, 3/16.xii.1916

МУЗЕЙ ВЪ АѲИНАХЪ.

— Всѣ старые портреты и статуи убрать!. У меня тутъ новые приготовлены.

In Greece, intrigues and counter-intrigues continued throughout 1916 between the neutralist or pro-German King Constantine XII/I and the pro-Allied statesman Eleftherios Venizelos, who had been dismissed as Prime Minister in the previous year. In the late summer of 1916, a Venizelist 'Committee of National Defence' was set up in Salonika. By December – the date of these cartoons – there were virtually two Greek governments: one loyal to the King controlling Athens and western Greece, and another which looked to Venizelos established in Salonika, controlling the east of the country and most of the islands; while substantial parts of Greece were in Allied military occupation, and the Allies were hectoring Constantine's government in various ways.

In this Russian cartoon, King Constantine is being instructed to replace portraits and statues in the Museum of Athens. He has been ordered to take down the portraits of Franz Josef and the King of Bulgaria, and is reluctantly removing the portrait of the Kaiser. He is being instructed to set up the portrait of his own pro-Allied brother, Prince George.

Cartoon 8.7 Still playing the slot machine. *San Francisco Chronicle*, San Francisco, 11.iii.1916

STILL PLAYING THE SLOT MACHINE

This American cartoon refers to Portugal's entry to the war on the Allied side in March 1916. Portugal had requisitioned German ships lying in her own European and colonial ports; this had been followed by a German declaration of war.

Mars – with a basket full of European belligerents – drops a 'scrap of paper' into the slot to get another one. The 'scrap of paper' allusion refers to the various international treaties which were supposed to have involved most of the nations down to that date. Whether 'scraps of paper' really played a major part in producing belligerents seems a good deal more doubtful today than it did to American observers in 1916; in any event there seems little reason for thinking that they played much part in involving Portugal.

9

Peace moves, 1916–17

By the early autumn of 1916, both sides were in a desperate condition. Germany, however, had one resource still untapped, which could perhaps give her victory, but which, if it failed, could equally well lead to her final defeat. If the submarine campaign could be stepped up to the limit, there was a chance that Britain – notoriously dependent on external supplies of food and raw materials – might be forced out of the war. As Britain was seen in Germany as the prime source of Allied finance, this would lead to general collapse of the Allies and a clear victory for the Central Powers.

Yet a policy of unrestricted submarine warfare would almost certainly bring the United States into the war on the Allied side. This had nearly happened earlier in the year. If America became a belligerent, it would take a considerable time to marshal her troops on to the European battle-fields; but, if they came, the numbers and the weapons would probably be enough to decide the war. It would, therefore, be a race between the submarines and the Americans.

The United States administration had long been anxious to bring about peace in Europe, and in the early part of 1916 important diplomatic efforts were made in that direction. Unfortunately, 1916 was a Presidential election year. Woodrow Wilson, of the Democratic Party, was President. He was seeking re-election, and voting would be held early in November. In the immediate run-up to that election, no man could speak with much authority for the United States, since nobody knew who would soon be President, or what policy he would follow. As it happened, Wilson was re-elected, but it was a close-run thing, and the result could not have been predicted with any confidence.

While the American election was moving towards its climax, important events were taking place in Germany. To over-simplify the issue considerably, the charismatic Kaiser largely withdrew from the centre of events, and the future direction of German policy became a matter of deep, though not public, dispute between what might be called the 'warmongers', headed by the military and naval leaders, and the 'peace-mongers', headed by Chancellor Theobald von Bethmann Hollweg. The peacemongers considered that there was a good chance that a peace on acceptable terms might be obtained through negotiations, with the United States doubtless playing a major part as mediator, while the warmongers favoured a fight to the finish, with every weapon at their disposal. Peacemongers and warmongers eventually moved to a sort of tacit compromise. A serious effort would be made to achieve an acceptable peace. If that failed, a full-scale submarine campaign would be unleashed.

The Allies probably had some idea of what was going on, and there was a sort of parallel to all this on their side, although the issues were less clear. A negotiated peace had obvious attractions, but some people thought that it was possible to win an outright victory.

On both sides, everything really turned on the minimum terms for a negotiated peace. As usually happens, each side was disposed to overestimate its own chances of winning outright victory at an acceptable cost, and therefore tended to pitch its 'war aims' too high. Perhaps peace negotiations were foredoomed from the start, but the story of their course is a remarkable one, on which cartoons cast considerable sidelights.

Cartoon 9.1 Death of the Emperor of Austria. *London Opinion*, London, 2.xii.1916

DEATH OF THE EMPEROR OF AUSTRIA.

THE KAISER: "Well, you did have the luck to die in your bed. I wonder whether I shall!"

In November 1916, Franz Josef, Emperor of Austria–Hungary, died and was succeeded by his thirty-year-old great-nephew Karl. This dynastic change would have considerable indirect influence on the subsequent course of the war.

In this cartoon, Wilhelm II stands by the catafalque, and muses on Franz Josef's good fortune. The shadowy noose in the background is indicative of a growing idea that the Kaiser, whom many regarded as personally responsible for the war, should be executed in the aftermath of victory: an early foretaste of the slogan 'Hang the Kaiser!' which would be raised in the British general election two years later.

The new Austro–Hungarian Emperor had a strong positive interest in peace negotiations. An early settlement would almost certainly provide the security required, with few or no territorial concessions, while delay would be bound to place increasing strains on the Empire, whatever the eventual upshot of the war might be.

Cartoon 9.2 Les Morts debout!!! *La Victoire,* Paris, 15.xii.1916

LES MORTS, DEBOUT !!!

par H.-G. IBELS

— LA PAIX, COMME ÇA!... NON, MAIS DES FOIS !!

Within a short time of Franz Josef's death, there were active moves for peace negotiations, which received strong encouragement from the new Emperor Karl, from the German Chancellor Bethmann Hollweg, and from the United States.

While the Allies found it impolitic to return a blunt refusal, they were not enthusiastic about the idea. In this French cartoon, the massive slaughter which had already occurred is advanced as a reason for continuing the war, not as a reason for making a compromise peace. The corpse of the dead soldier rises from his grave to refuse the German offer. The implication is that acceptance of the offer would be a betrayal of the dead, 'Peace like that! . . . No, never!!' declares the dead man.

Cartoon 9.3 Of two evils the lesser. *The Bystander,*
London, 27.xii.1916

Of Two Evils the Lesser

In Britain, there was a major political crisis in December 1916. The intentions of the various participants in that crisis have been widely disputed ever since, but the upshot was that Prime Minister Asquith was replaced by Lloyd George. It is often thought that the essential question at stake was the manner in which the war was to be fought rather than whether peace negotiations should be entered, and Asquith himself seems to have been as eager to continue the war as his successor was. There were, however, important voices being raised in Britain which seemed to favour peace negotiations, and the present cartoon suggests that the new Prime Minister would resist such ideas to the limit.

Lloyd George is seated in a railway carriage between Bellona, goddess of war, and a type-cast German with the caged dove of a 'German peace'. In the luggage rack above their heads, each of the three passengers has luggage. Bellona has shells and high explosives, Lloyd George has the 'Good Wishes of the Empire', the German has the various territories currently occupied by the Central Powers. Lloyd George prefers Bellona to his other companion. He carries 'the mantle of Pitt', recognising that Pitt, too, had led Britain and her Allies in pursuing a warlike policy at a time when a prolonged negotiated peace appeared to be a real possibility.

Cartoon 9.4 A Japanese view of peace. *Jiji*, Tokyo, copied in *New York Tribune*, 23.i.1917

(*From Jiji, Tokio*)

Germany: "Look here! It's the year-end bargain. The asking price may be a bit fancy, but it won't hurt you to look at it, will it?"

The belligerents were encouraged, particularly by the United States, to declare their war aims. All pitched those war aims at a level higher than they could realistically hope to receive – just like people almost anywhere haggling over a price. In the Japanese cartoon, the Kaiser points that fact out, almost furtively, to the Allies. He was, of course, vulnerable to criticism at home which would have destroyed his authority if he had been seen to offer over-generous terms, particularly in the early phase of negotiations.

Cartoon 9.5 The Kaiser's birthday party.
Star, London, 27.i.1917

HINDENBURG (to von Capelle): "Oh, let him talk."

This British cartoon suggests that warmongers on the side of the Central Powers did not anticipate that the peace negotiations would achieve success. The Kaiser no longer appears – as he usually does in Allied cartoons – as the principal bogey-man for the Allies. The sincerity of his advocacy of peace does not seem to be impugned, and his son, Crown Prince Wilhelm ('Little Willie') endorses his father's proposals. King Ferdinand of Bulgaria and the Sultan are weary and sceptical; but the new Emperor Karl of Austria–Hungary (centre right) looks more interested.

Paul von Hindenburg, the chief army leader, and Edward von Capelle, who had succeeded von Tirpitz as Minister of Marine, view proceedings with cynicism, confident that the war would continue.

Cartoon 9.6 E.R.F.I. & Co. G.m.b.H. *Fliegende Blätter,* Munich, 19.i.1917

E. R. F. I. & Co.
G. m. b. H.
Meine Herren, nur schnell hinunter damit, sonst
geht unser Geschäft pleite.

Strohfeuer.

| Am allerleichtesten verdammt, | Am schnellsten aber das, was er |
| Wer sich für alles rasch entflammt, | Begeistert pries noch kurz vorher. |

O. E. W.

This German cartoon apeared in mid-January 1917, at a time when it was fairly clear that the peace negotiations had failed. President Poincaré of France and John Bull lift the coffin of the 'German Angel of Peace' into its grave, with a Russian and King Victor Emmanuel III of Italy assisting. The four are cast as undertakers belonging to the firm 'E(ngland) R(ussia) F(rance) I(taly) Ltd.'. John Bull addresses the others: 'Gentlemen, now down with it quickly, or else our business will go bankrupt.'

Cartoon 9.7 Budem kak Dikari! *Novoe Vremya,* Petrograd, 25.ii./10.iii.1917

«БУДЕМЪ, КАКЪ ДИКАРИ!»

— Впередъ, Германія!

When it became certain that the Allies would not accept the German peace offer, Germany announced her decision to engage in unrestricted submarine warfare.

This Russian cartoon, which appeared when the first rumblings of the revolution were already being heard, expresses the general judgement of the Allies and of the United States on the matter. Germania and a barbarian tribesman endorse the title: 'We will be like savages!' 'Forward, Germania!' is the message at the bottom of the cartoon.

10

Revolution in Russia: stage 1

Great events which have long been predicted tend to take everybody by surprise when at last they occur. The first phase of the Russian Revolution was an event of that kind.

Innumerable cartoons from various countries had testified over many years to the view that the political system over which the Russian Tsar presided must either reform or perish in revolution. That message was clearly formulated not only in the reign of Nicholas II but also in that of his father Alexander III; while his grandfather Alexander II had died horribly through the action of a politically motivated assassin.

When war broke out in 1914, both sides gave great weight to the probable effect of Russia on the course of the conflict. It was the fear of Russia that Germany and Austria–Hungary entertained which turned a Balkan dispute into a general European war. The western Allies spoke enthusiastically of the 'Russian steamroller' which would play a decisive part in events.

Two and a half years on, Russia had lost enormous numbers of men and considerable slices of territory, but the system over which the Tsar presided showed little sign of imminent collapse. It would be difficult to find evidence at the beginning of March 1917 which suggested that anybody anywhere anticipated that a fundamental change in the structure of the country was little over a fortnight away.

The crucial chain of events began with bread riots in Petrograd on 8 March. They seemed to pose no threat to the régime, and on the same day the Tsar departed from the city to visit the headquarters of his army, far away. In the next couple of days, the disturbances grew much more severe. On 9 March, a special conference of the Duma, or Parliament, was called to deal with the matter of food supplies. On 10 March, there were serious clashes between rioters and armed police. On 12 March, the Tsar issued a ukase forbidding the Duma to meet. On the same day it met nevertheless, and established an Executive Committee.

On 14 March, two dramatic events occurred. The Petrograd Council (Soviet, in Russian) of Workers' and Soldiers' Delegates was established; and the Executive Committee of the Duma claimed to take over government of the Russian Empire.

In the course of the next couple of days, even greater events followed in quick succession. The Executive Committee of the Duma appointed a Provisional Government under Prince George Lvov, which promptly urged the Tsar to abdicate in favour of his ailing young son, Alexei. The Tsar, apparently for reasons of paternal solicitude, refused, but he offered instead to abdicate in favour of his brother, the Grand Duke Michael. Michael refused to accept in the circumstances; thus on 16 March, the Tsar's abdication took place without a successor being named. Thus far, however, no move was taken to establish a republic, although it was decided that a constituent assembly should be summoned. Criticism was directed against Nicholas, not against the political system over which he presided.

Meanwhile, the Soviet issued its Order No. 1, declaring the army to be subject to itself. Establishment of the Petrograd Soviet was soon followed by similar bodies in other parts of the Empire. For some time there existed a curious relationship between the Duma and the Soviets; sometimes uneasy, but sometimes quite friendly. Alexander Kerensky, who would later achieve great importance, contrived to be a high official of both bodies without any apparent clash of loyalties.

At this point there was no suggestion from either the Provisional Government or the Soviets that Russia should withdraw from the war. Very soon, however, ordinary Russian and German soldiers began to fraternise, but the extent of that fraternisation, and its likely implications, were far from clear. It is important to remember that at this stage of the war the Bolsheviks were of negligible importance, not only in the dealings of the Duma and the Provisional Government, but also in the Soviets.

The events which brought down the Tsar lasted, from start to finish, just over a week. The major Russian press largely shut down during the turmoil, and there was much uncertainty in foreign countries as to just what was happening, Cartoons, therefore, can tell little about the actual stages of the critical period; but they can tell much about how matters seemed immediately beforehand, and how they seemed shortly after the Tsar had fallen.

Cartoon 10.1 Der Zar auf der Leiche Rasputins. *Simplicissimus*, Munich, 23.i.1917

Der Zar auf der Leiche Rasputins

Verwaist — —

frei nach Klinger

The Tsar crouches by the body of the murdered Rasputin. The drawing parodies a painting by Max Klinger, and the word at the foot of the cartoon means 'Orphaned'.

Rasputin, a 'holy man' generally known under a nickname which means 'immoral', may have been mystic, charlatan or both; but he certainly acquired great influence over the Tsarina, who believed that he was capable of healing her haemophiliac son. That influence extended to the Tsar as well, and ranged over political matters. It was widely believed that Rasputin supported German peace moves. This led to his murder, just before the end of 1916, by a group of Russian aristocrats. The Tsar, the cartoonist suggests, was unhinged by this event, and incapable of taking effective decisions.

Cartoon 10.2 The portent. *New York World,* New York, 18.iii.1917

THE PORTENT

These two cartoons – one from a strongly pro-Allied newspaper in a technically neutral country, and one from Germany – both rejoice at the same event: the fall of the Russian Tsar.

The *New York World* approves of the fall of the Tsar, and suggests that the Russian Revolution portends similar events in Germany.

Der Brummer shows the Tsar being pulled down – perhaps into the flames of hell? – and appends a text from Heine, 'There falls a hoar-frost in a spring night'.

Cartoon 10.3 Die Revolution in Russland. *Der Brummer*, Berlin, ca. 22.iii.1917

Die Revolution in Rußland. Es fiel ein „Reif" in Frühlingsnacht. — (Heine)

Cartoon 10.4 Indignation. *Le Canard Enchaîné,* Paris, 18.iv.1917

INDIGNATION

— *Quelle horreur! Cachez ça! Nous ne l'avons jamais connu!*

This very cynical French cartoon of April 1917 comments on the ease with which Allied politicans 'forgot' their previous association with the deposed Tsar. 'Dreadful thing! Hide it! We've never known him!' they cry, as the portrait of Nicholas is displayed. Among the politicians portrayed are Théophile Delcassé, a former Foreign Minister, and Georges Clémenceau, who was to play a major part in French politics in the last year of the war.

There is some force in the cartoonist's criticism. In the earlier part of the war, while the Tsar was in office, few important Allied politicians offered much public criticism of Nicholas; once he fell from power they acclaimed the new regime as a liberation.

11

America enters the war

At the very moment when Tsarism in Russia was moving towards its final collapse, the United States of America was preparing to enter the conflict on the Allied side.

Throughout January 1917, President Wilson continued to labour for peace negotiations, and it was in that month that he coined the slogan 'Peace without Victory'. But the German decision to resume unrestricted submarine warfare as from 1 February was followed almost immediately by a general assumption in the United States that the country would soon be at war.

On 3 February, before there had been time to see how the new submarine policy would work in practice, the United States formally severed diplomatic relations with Germany. At the beginning of March, the Zimmermann telegram, which had been intercepted by the British and disclosed to the American government some weeks earlier, was made public. This revealed that Alfred Zimmermann, the German Foreign Minister, had been attempting to incite Mexico and Japan against the United States.

On 18 March, three American merchant ships were sunk by German submarines. Two days later, the President called for an American declaration of war. Under the United States constitution, this step required Congressional approval, and so special sessions were summoned early in April. Vast majorities of both Houses approved the President's recommendation, and war was declared on 6 April.

The almost simultaneous fall of the Tsar and involvement of the United States – widely seen as most democratic of all major countries – seemed to change the whole character of the war. Before that date, people on the Allied side had tended to see the war as a struggle for specific objectives, like the liberation of Belgium or Serbia, or the ownership of Alsace and Lorraine. Thereafter, it came to be regarded more and more as a war fought for ideological principles like democracy; or the right of all peoples to self-government; or the establishment of a new international order based on the rule of law rather than force. To some people, it even became 'the war to end war'. The fact that these high objectives were

85

not realised in the aftermath of war does not mean that the people who proclaimed them while the war was being fought were necessarily hypocrites.

Cartoon 11.1 A bunch of Neros. *San Francisco Chronicle,* San Francisco, 23.i.1917

⊛⊛⊛   A BUNCH OF NEROS   ⊛⊛⊛

Throughout January 1917, opinion in the United States tended to be highly critical of both sides in the war, while Allied opinion was deeply sceptical of the United States.

In this cartoon, the *San Francisco Chronicle* sees the Europeans on both sides as 'a bunch of Neros' – fiddling while Rome (or in this case, all Europe) is burning.

Cartoon 11.2 Can he mend it again?
Chicago Tribune, 11.ii.1917

CAN HE MEND IT AGAIN?

At the end of January 1917 the Germans had evidently despaired of peace negotiations taking place, and announced unrestricted submarine warfare. This announcement was of crucial importance in shifting American opinion towards the view that the United States must soon enter the war on the Allied side, and (as already seen) was followed swiftly by severance of diplomatic relations between the two countries.

This cartoon appeared rather more than a week later. The German Emperor is the little boy who has shattered America's friendship. The cartoonist asks, perhaps not very hopefully, whether he can mend it again.

Cartoon 11.3 Exploding in his hands.
New York World, 3.iii.1917

EXPLODING IN HIS HANDS

At the beginning of March 1917, German–American relations took a further downward turn with disclosure of the Zimmermann telegram – in this cartoon called simply a 'note'.

The United States had been on bad terms with Mexico for some time, and the telegram contained an offer of United States territories which had belonged to Mexico long before. Publication of the Zimmermann telegram was important in persuading many Americans that Germany was fostering designs against their own country.

Cartoon 11.4 Wall Street's war call. *Irish World,* New York, 31.iii.1917

WALL STREET'S WAR CALL
Wall Street—"Come to the Trenches and Fight for My Loans."
Columbia—"This Is My Banner."

This cartoon appeared later in March 1917, soon after President Wilson appealed to Congress to declare war on Germany. The great majority of American periodicals endorsed the President's views, but the *Irish World* was an exception.

The cartoonist suggests that the primary reason for America's developing involvement was her close financial links with Britain, and that 'Wall Street' – that is, the New York stock exchange – was at the root of it.

90

Cartoon 11.5 To the Defense of his Standard!
Chicago Tribune, 4.iv.1917

TO THE DEFENSE OF HIS STANDARD!

[Copyright: 1917: By John T. McCutcheon.]

This cartoon appeared a couple of days before the United States declared war, but at a time when the matter was a foregone conclusion. The war was seen as a conflict between Democracy and Autocracy, in which Uncle Sam was being welcomed by his natural associates. The comparison would have been impossible a month earlier, for the Tsar had been deposed less than three weeks beforehand.

Cartoon 11.6 Then up he came ... *The Passing Show,* London, 28.iv.1917

Drawn by G. E. Studdy.

THEN UP HE CAME WITH *HIS* LITTLE LOT!

John Bull sits fishing for U-boats. Uncle Sam arrives to help, accompanied by 'his little lot'. A number of Latin American states also took the occasion to declare war on Germany.

92

12

A time of waiting

Within a space of just over two months in the early part of 1917 there had occurred three events of first magnitude, any one of which might reasonably have been expected to determine the whole outcome of the war. On 1 February the Germans resumed unrestricted submarine warfare; on 16 March the Russian Tsardom collapsed; and on 6 April the United States declared war against Germany. Most of the important things which happened in connection with the war during the remainder of 1917 had their roots in one or more of those three events.

In a sense, there was not much that anybody could usefully do so far as the land war was concerned, but wait. Great offensives certainly took place in 1917; but there was little reason even at the time for thinking that any of them could win the war for either side. In that sense they were different from the offensives of earlier years, which the military planners really seem to have conceived as war-winning activities.

Indeed, the offensives tended to be counter-productive for the Powers which launched them. The French offensive in Champagne in the spring led to near-mutiny, which was only contained when General Nivelle was replaced by General – later Marshal – Pétain, whose strategy was of a more defensive kind. The unsuccessful Russian offensive in Eastern Galicia in July may have been of crucial importance in fostering the demoralisation of Russian troops which led to the second phase of the revolution in the autumn. That matter, however, will be considered in a later chapter. The Southern Front in the Italian borders yielded little benefit to the Allied attackers, and produced the Italian fiasco of Caporetto in October.

The Central Powers, by contrast, were more shrewd. Advances they certainly made on the Eastern Front; but these advances were achieved against an enemy which was already disintegrating. The real issue on all the European land fronts was whether the Allies could hold the line until American soldiers and equipment arrived in numbers sufficient to turn the scale.

A few new belligerents appeared, all on the Allied side. The disposition of Latin American countries to declare war on Germany in the wake of the United States has already been noted. King Constantine of Greece was deposed in June, and later in the month that country also rallied to the Allied side. In August, China declared war on the Central Powers. None of these interventions seems to have produced any significant effect on the course of the war.

The war at sea was of crucial importance. Everything turned on how effective 'unrestricted submarine warfare' would be, and how soon. If it worked, Britain would be forced out of the war by starvation, or by failure of some other kind of vital supplies, and the lynchpin of the whole Allied machine would snap. Even the limitless reserves of men, materials and finance from the United States would prove unavailing. To counter this fearful menace, the British gave more general attention to the war against U-boats, and in particular they developed the convoy system.

This change of naval strategy involved great changes of outlook. Admirals believed in battleships, not in submarines and destroyers; and it was with great reluctance that they accepted the idea of convoys. It is arguable that the German failure to put more emphasis on submarines and less on capital ships, lost them the Great War – and perhaps the war of 1939–45 as well.

The twelve months from December 1916 to November 1917 witnessed important changes at high levels of government, closely related to the direction of the war, in all major European belligerent countries. The replacement of Asquith by Lloyd George in Britain and the first phase of the Russian Revolution have already been noted; the second phase of the Russian Revolution will be considered in a later chapter. In Austria–Hungary and Germany, there were changes at the highest levels of government. In France, the appointment of Georges Clémenceau as premier in November 1917 was an event of great importance both for the direction of the war and for the character of the eventual peace treaties.

Cartoon 12.1 Hindenburg, der 'Lorbeerhamster', *Kladderadatsch*, Berlin, 30.ix.1917

Hindenburg, der „Lorbeerhamster"

In 1917, most of the significant military victories were won by Germany, although none of these victories was to prove decisive.

In this German cartoon, 'Hindenburg, the laurel-hoarder' is so smothered with the laurels of victory that he is barely visible. In the latter part of the war Hindenburg, more than any other man, was seen as a sort of father-figure, the very epitome of victory. The labels on the laurels refer to actual victories won by Hindenburg at various stages in the Great War.

A little, half-humorous ribbon at the bottom extends the good wishes of 'Dr Kladd', representing *Kladderadatsch*. It was common for satirical periodicals to use a small, comic figure to represent 'editorial' opinion. 'Mr Punch' was the most famous, though not the only, corresponding British figure. 'Dr Kladd' had appeared at intervals over many years.

Cartoon 12.2 A la frontière italienne. *Le Journal,*
Paris, 30.x.1917

A LA FRONTIERE ITALIENNE

LE POILU FRANÇAIS. — *Tiens bon, [...] me voici : le Boche, c'est un peu
mon rayon...*
(Dessin de Radiguet.)

Although Italy had been at war with Austria–Hungary since the spring
of 1915, war was not declared on Germany until August 1916. The tide
of war on the southern front soon shifted in favour of the Central Powers,
and this culminated in the Italian disaster at Caporetto in October 1917.
Thereafter it was decided that French troops should be sent to buttress
the Italians, and an Allied Supreme War Council was established. The
Anglo-French strategy of bringing Italy into the war to relieve pressure
on other Allies had not merely failed, but proved counter-productive.

This French cartoon makes the best of the situation. In the background,
the Italian is being worsted by the German, and an Austrian comes up
the hill. The French *poilu* shouts, 'Hold on, friend, here I am: the Boche
is rather my business.'

96

Cartoon 12.3 La prise de Jérusalem. *La Victoire,*
Paris, 13.xii.1917

LA PRISE DE JERUSALEM

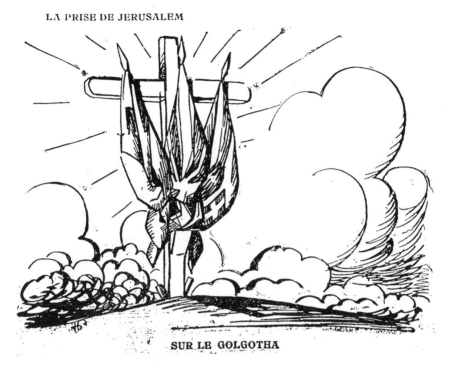

SUR LE GOLGOTHA

In the autumn of 1917, Allied troops advanced into the Ottoman province
of Palestine, and in December they captured Jerusalem. This victory was,
perhaps, of more symbolic than military value; but it signalled the gradual
collapse of Ottoman power in Arab lands. Promises were made to Arabs
and Jews alike, and in this period the Zionist aspiration of a Jewish home-
land in Palestine and the Arab aspiration of independence from the Turks
both began to seem politically realistic.

This French cartoon commemorates the taking of Jerusalem. The Cross,
draped with French, British and Italian flags, is raised on Golgotha, site
of the Crucifixion. The religious significance of the event was strong,
particularly in the approach to Christmas. Did the cartoonist perhaps also
reflect on the meaning of the name: 'the place of the skull'?

Cartoon 12.4 Making rapid strides. *John Bull*, London, 11.viii.1917

MAKING RAPID STRIDES.

UNCLE SAM: "Hold the fort, for I am coming!"

Just as it had proved necessary to bring German troops into the Italian theatre of war to help the Austro-Hungarians, and French troops to help the Italians, so were all the Allies really doing little more than holding on in the land war in anticipation of the eventual arrival of Americans.

This *John Bull* cartoon expresses the situation bluntly. The Americans were 'making rapid strides' in organising great armies in the course of 1917, but they would not arrive in Europe until the following year.

Cartoon 12.5 Davy Jones knows. *Montreal Daily Star*, Montreal, 5.xi.1917

DAVY JONES KNOWS

One well-known party who can answer Germany's bluffing question: "Where is the British Navy?"

In the course of 1917, a highly effective campaign against German U-boats accompanied an equally effective campaign of 'damage limitation' through the use of naval convoys. 'Davy Jones', at the bottom of the sea, gloats over the submarines which have fallen into his 'locker'. This was of crucial importance to Britain, and perhaps to the whole Allied cause.

Cartoon 12.6 Cold feet. *The Passing Show,* London, 15.xii.1917

COLD FEET.

The Snowman (*to Lord Lansdowne*): "YOU ARE TOO HANDY WITH YOUR WHITE FLAG, MY LORD; MUCH TOO HANDY."
Lansdowne: "B-B-BUT THINGS ARE SO V-V-VERY S-S-SERIOUS."
Snowman: "I'M YES—BUT IT'S NOT THE FIRST TIME YOU HAVE HOISTED IT, IT SEEMS TO BE A POSITIVE HOBBY OF YOURS."

The Marquess of Lansdowne, as Foreign Secretary, had played a major part in bringing about the Anglo-French *entente cordiale* in 1903–4. He served in Asquith's Coalition cabinet, but left the Government when Lloyd George took office in December 1916. Towards the end of 1917, he wrote a letter to the *Daily Telegraph*, implying the possibility of peace negotiations.

This cartoon savagely attacks Lansdowne for displaying the 'white flag' of surrender. As the paper in Lansdowne's pocket suggests, the cartoonist also attacks him for his action over the House of Lords crisis in 1911.

Lansdowne's politics were strongly Conservative (or, more technically, 'Unionist'). The spectators who are portrayed cheering him, however, were of very different politics. Ramsay MacDonald, to the left of the picture, and Philip Snowden, were members of the Labour Party. The *Daily News* was a Liberal newspaper. R. L. Outhwaite, to the right of the picture, was a Liberal MP who was a particular enthusiast for land taxing, and had won a sensational by-election victory from Labour in 1912.

100

Cartoon 12.7 Un ministère homogène. *Le Canard Enchaîné*, Paris, 28.xi.1917

UN MINISTÈRE HOMOGÈNE

LE MINISTRE DE LA GUERRE (Pᵗ DU CONSEIL)

LE MINISTRE DE LA JUSTICE

LE MINISTRE DE LA MARINE

LE MINISTRE DE L'INSTRUCTION PUBLIQUE

LE MINISTRE DES FINANCES

LE MINISTRE DES AFFAIRES ÉTRANGÈRES

LE MINISTRE DE L'INTERIEUR

LE MINISTRE DU TRAVAIL

Georges Clémenceau had earned the nickname 'the tiger' long before the war for his skill in demolishing French governments. His political attitudes were highly individualistic, and at different times he had earned enthusiastic support, and bitter criticism, from more conventional politicians of 'right' and 'left' alike.

When war came, Clémenceau's devotion to the cause of victory was not in doubt. By November 1917, when he was appointed head of government by President Poincaré, morale was low, both in the forces and among civilians.

This French cartoon comments on the new Ministry which Clémenceau formed. It was predictable from the start that the new Premier would not adopt the role of mere chairman of a committee; he would dominate the Ministry. As the cartoon suggests, Clémenceau was indeed both President of the Council (Premier) and Minister of War. The cartoonist goes further, and suggests that he was performing most of the other important jobs in the government as well.

13

Revolution in Russia: stage 2

The general enthusiasm, particularly in the Allied camp, which greeted the fall of the Tsar and the establishment of a 'Provisional Government' in Russia, in March 1917 appears to have been sincere. It was widely believed that the change of government would result in much more vigorous prosecution of the war, as well as removing the political embarrassment of having a major Ally governed by a corrupt and tyrannical regime.

Almost immediately, however, there were clear signs that Russian soldiers had no more wish to fight for the new government than for the old. Fraternisation between soldiers on the two sides of the Eastern Front became widespread, and Russian discipline was palpably breaking down – whatever the Provisional Government, or even the Soviets, might wish.

In May 1917 the Petrograd government itself broke step with the other Allies. While the idea of a separate peace with Germany was repudiated firmly, the new Government called for a peace without annexations or indemnities: a proposal highly disconcerting for Frenchmen who yearned for the restoration of Alsace and Lorraine, or for heavy compensation for damage done to their country.

In June, the first meeting of the All-Russian Congress of Soviets was held. It celebrated the occasion by demanding the abolition of the Duma. At the turn of June and July, the last great Russian offensive was launched, in Galicia. After initial success, it proved a disastrous failure. The unsuccessful offensive was followed by the 'July Days', which were marked by violent mass demonstrations in Petrograd. The Provisional Government was able to restore order, and outlawed the Bolsheviks, who were seen as chief agents of the disturbances. Another important change soon followed, for Alexander Kerensky replaced Prince Lvov as head of government.

A couple of months after the Galician failure, the army sustained another major military disaster at Riga: an event which seems due at least in part to the general unwillingness of Russian soldiers to fight. About the same time, a certain General Kornilov ordered his troops to march on the capital. The move failed, and in any case there was doubt as to

Kornilov's motives, but thereafter the Provisional Government's authority was rapidly sapped. Workers began to take over factories, peasants began seizing estates, and soldiers deserted, largely in order to be in on any land partitioning which might take place. The Ukraine and Finland became more or less independent states.

September witnessed formal declaration of a republic, while the Bolsheviks won control of the Petrograd and Moscow Soviets. In October the Bolshevik leader Lenin, who had fled a few months earlier, returned to Petrograd.

Early in November, the Bolshevik threat became very serious, and Kerensky sought to suppress the Bolshevik press. Troops hostile to the government, and 'Red Guards', were called out. With very little bloodshed Petrograd (St Petersburg) fell to the Bolsheviks, the Winter Palace was stormed and most of the Provisional Government arrested. By the night of 7 November, the Bolsheviks were in control of the capital.

Cartoon 13.1 Der russische Tanzbär ... *Der Brummer*, Berlin, No. 151 (about 26.vii.1917)

Der russische Tanzbär will nicht mehr. Zum Teufel! Ich tanze nicht länger nach deiner Pfeife!

In June 1917, the last major Russian offensive was launched in Galicia. It proved a costly failure. Thereafter the ordinary Russian soldiers evinced less and less eagerness to continue fighting.

In this German cartoon, 'The Russian dancing bear has had enough!', the Briton discovers to his astonishment that the bear is refusing to dance – despite the music which was being played and the bag of gold which was offered. The bear, with 'Russian people' on its cap, is emphatic on the point: 'Go to the devil! I shall not dance any longer to your pipes!'

Cartoon 13.2 Moloch. *Rabochy Pyt (Pravda)*, Petrograd, 22.ix/5.x.1917

МОЛОХЪ.

Шаржъ рис. А. З.

Полюбуйтесь на банкира,
Почему онъ противъ мира.
У чудовища Молоха

Онъ устроился не плохо.
У Молоха пасть раскрыта —
Родъ бездоннаго корыта.

Всѣхъ сожралъ-бы онъ живьемъ
— Подпишитесь на заемъ!

М. В.

By the end of September, the Bolsheviks were becoming a major force in the Soviets of Russian cities.

This Bolshevik cartoon comments bitterly on the Russian war effort. A soldier and a peasant feed a million roubles into the mouth of the Moloch 'War'. Money which the idol had previously consumed is being voided into the pocket of the banker. 'Nice for the banker – which is why he is against peace', the poem begins. The war is represented as a 'rich man's war', which costs the poor much, but from which they derive no benefit.

105

Cartoon 13.3 The pirate's opportunity. *John Bull,* London, 17.xi.1917

THE PIRATE'S OPPORTUNITY.

"The Struggle for the Wheel."

This cartoon appeared in November 1917, shortly after the Bolshevik takeover in Petrograd, but long before it was clear that the Bolsheviks would be able, even temporarily, to secure control of the rest of Russia.

Kerensky and a Bolshevik struggle for the wheel of Russia, while the Kaiser, dressed as a pirate, climbs aboard to seize the ship of state for his own advantage. The principal interest of this British cartoonist (and probably of most people in Allied countries) was not in whether or not Bolshevism triumphed in Russia, but in whether Germany was able to derive some advantage from the confusion.

Cartoon 13.4 Mirnoe Chaepitie. *Pravda*, Petrograd, 19.xi./2.xii.1917

This Bolshevik cartoon, 'Peaceful tea-drinking', appeared a few weeks after the take-over in Petrograd. It shows two Russians drinking tea together, and casually discussing politics. One complains, 'The Ministers haven't done anything.' On the wall are posters referring to the decree on land and the decree on peace, which were issued on 8 November, the day after the Bolsheviks took power.

The Decree on Land declared the immediate abolition of great landed estates, without compensation, and passed them to local agrarian committees and peasants' soviets. The decree on peace extended an immediate offer of peace without annexation or indemnities.

14

Revolution in Russia: Stage 3

Before November 1917 was out, the new Bolshevik government of Russia ordered cessation of hostilities against the Central Powers. In mid-December an armistice was formally concluded at Brest–Litovsk.

At the very beginning of the life of the Bolshevik government, many Western observers probably regarded it as not wildly different from its predecessor.

Yet even before negotiations at Brest–Litovsk were completed, it became clear that the Bolshevik government was becoming a highly repressive regime, which rapidly suppressed civil liberties, and developed the familiar apparatus of an omnipresent secret police. External observers, whether in the camp of the Allies or of the Central Powers, soon experienced an even deeper anxiety. The Bolsheviks perceived their revolution as the spark which would ignite world revolution. At the masthead of their main periodical, *Pravda*, were the ominous words, 'Proletariat of all lands, unite!'

Many incidents, both in the Allied countries and in the Central Powers, had suggested that working people were becoming increasingly unwilling to fight a war from which they anticipated no benefit, and also that they were coming to ask radical questions about the economic and social order. These rebels were not, for the most part, 'Bolsheviks' in any ordinary sense of the term, but they might well become so if sufficient encouragement were given.

From December 1917 until early March 1918, peace negotiations proceeded at Brest–Litovsk. There were many deep disputes – some of them between the Bolshevik leaders themselves – but the upshot was the Treaty of Brest–Litovsk, concluded on 3 March. Large tracts of the former Russian Empire were annexed by the Central Powers, and the Ukraine became, for practical purposes, a German satellite.

The concern of the Central Powers at Brest–Litovsk was plain enough: to secure as much territory as possible; to remove any need for keeping large numbers of troops in the east, so that everything could be pitched into the Western Front; and to secure ample supplies of food and materials to counter the Allied blockade.

The Russian concern was more complex. Certainly it was vital to end a fearfully destructive war which there was no hope of winning, but there was also an important element of political theory in the transaction. Lenin had convinced himself that all major belligerents were more or less ripe for socialist revolution, and that it was merely a matter of time until those revolutions should take place. On that assumption, it mattered little just which former Russian territories became independent, or were ceded to the Central Powers. It was only important that a sufficient nucleus should be preserved to initiate the impending world revolution. It was the function of the Bolsheviks (or Communists, as they were now becoming known) to organise what remained of Russia to achieve that historical mission.

In one sense, this attitude may be perceived as altruism on a grand scale; but in another sense it was nothing of the kind. Revolution, the Bolshevik philosophy ran, is indivisible. Either world revolution must take place, or the revolution in Russia must be destroyed, and presumably members of the Bolshevik government with it. Some opponents of Bolshevism, both inside and outside Russia, were attracted to the same philosophy, but drew from it the inspiration for a very different course of action.

At the time of the Treaty of Brest–Litovsk, the future of those parts of the former Russian Empire which were not annexed, or dominated, by the Central Powers was still profoundly uncertain. The Bolsheviks had established control over much – perhaps over most – of 'Russia', in the narrow sense of that word, but were by no means unchallenged, and they would soon encounter formidable opposition from various counter-revolutionary, or 'white', armies.

From the point of view of Britain, France and the United States, the overwhelming need was to deny the large stores of military equipment, and the mineral and agricultural wealth, of the area to the Central Powers. Japan shared these interests, but to a smaller extent. Her primary concern was to seize, or to dominate economically, what she could of Russian territory in the Far East.

The Allies soon came to be involved in the imbroglio in various ways, and not always on the same side. At about the time of the Treaty of Brest–Litovsk, there were large military stores in northern Russia which might perhaps fall into German hands. The Allies and the Bolsheviks had a common interest to prevent this happening, and the Allies intervened, with Bolshevik approval, to stave off the Germans.

In April 1918, however, British, American and Japanese troops landed at Vladivostok. Here again substantial military stores existed. The Allies can hardly have feared that the Germans would have been able to seize those stores from such a remote spot, but there was (in theory at least) some danger that the Bolsheviks might be prepared to offer war materials to the Germans in exchange for advantages elsewhere. No doubt the Japanese were intervening in order to secure territorial advantage; perhaps an important consideration for the Anglo-Saxon Allies was to prevent them doing anything of the kind.

The Allies also began to become involved in other parts of the Russian fringe. In the summer of 1918, active civil war flared up in parts of the former Russian Empire, and the Allies began to intervene with the object of supporting 'white' against 'red' forces. This intervention appears to have been inspired mainly by the belief that the 'whites' would be more likely than the 'reds' to deny materials to the Central Powers; but some influential people on the Allied side were already beginning to fear that the Bolshevik precedent might be emulated in other countries, and were anxious to stamp out Bolshevism as soon as possible.

Another quite separate group of pro-Allied soldiers also played a substantial part in the story. At a much earlier stage of the war, considerable numbers of Czechs and Slovaks who had been enrolled in the armies of Austria–Hungary had defected to the Russian side, and by the time of the Bolshevik revolution were to be found in more or less discrete Czecho–Slovak military units.

The Czechs and Slovaks had reason to fear that if they returned to their own country while the war was in progress, they would be treated as soldiers who defect to the enemy side are generally treated in all armies. They needed to stay together in more or less distinct units, and try to work their way eastwards towards the Pacific, in the hope that they would eventually be returned to their own country in the aftermath of an Allied victory. In the meantime they were compelled to live on the country, which necessarily brought them into conflict with Russian authorities, but their overriding concern was with their own future, not with the course of political events in Russia.

Cartoon 14.1 Der Weltgläubiger. *Simplicissimus,*
Munich, 18.xii.1917

Der Weltgläubiger   (16. 16. Seine)

„Halt — halt — der Bär gehört mir!"

This German cartoon of December 1917 comments both on the commence-
ment of peace negotiations between Germany and Russia at Brest–Litovsk,
and the role of the United States, which has become (in the words of the
title), 'The world-creditor'.

The angel of peace gently carries away the happy-looking Russian bear
from the ravaged countryside. President Wilson seeks to restrain the bear,
shouting 'Stop! Stop! The bear belongs to me!'.

This cartoon may be contrasted with the earlier German cartoon 5.3,
in which Britain rather than the United States is seen as the general cred-
itor. The war was already imposing a great strain on Britain's financial
position, which had been overwhelmingly strong at the beginning.

111

Cartoon 14.2 Rectifying the frontiers. *New York World,* New York, 24.ii.1918

"RECTIFYING THE FRONTIERS."

Peace negotiations between German and Russian representatives at Brest–Litovsk continued for nearly three months. Both sides, however, had reason to bring them to a conclusion as quickly as possible. The Central Powers were anxious to turn to the Western Front without fear of distraction, before the Americans arrived in force. The Bolsheviks wished to be free to organise what was left to them as a Communist state.

This American cartoon appeared about a week before negotiations were complete, but when the general outline of the settlement was fairly clear. The German Emperor is 'rectifying the frontiers' by seizing great tracts of Russia.

Cartoon 14.3 Le Gâteau russe. *Le Journal*, Paris, 2.iii.1918

LE GATEAU RUSSE

— Voici ta part, jeune Ostro-Karl, et apprends qu'en arithmétique allemande deux moitiés ne sont jamais égales. (Dessin de LUCIEN MÉTIVET.)

Germany and Austria–Hungary are dividing 'the Russian cake'. Wilhelm allocates only a tiny fragment to Karl, pointing out 'that in German arithmetic, two halves are never equal'.

Cartoon 14.4 Delivering the goods. *The Bystander,*
London, 27.ii.1918

DELIVERING THE GOODS

What might be called the 'official' views of the Treaty of Brest–Litovsk from the two sides are indicated in these cartoons (14.4 and 14.5).

The British view, expressed in *The Bystander*, shows the Bolshevik leaders Lenin and Trotsky handing over a gigantic manacled Russian to the Kaiser, who apparently proposes to hang him. The Bolsheviks receive, in return, 'the price', (A French cartoon, which appeared in *La Victoire* a few days later, which probably took its idea from *The Bystander* but varied the incident slightly, is more specific. Trotsky holds a bag containing the Biblical 'thirty pieces of silver'.) The German view, expressed in *Fliegende Blätter*, shows a kindly Michel binding up the wounded paw of the Russian bear – the beginning, perhaps, of a beautiful friendship.

The two views are equally unconvincing. It is difficult to see how anybody, whether representing the Tsardom, the Provisional Government or the Bolsheviks, could have induced most of the Russian soldiers to fight any more, and the Germans were therefore for practical purposes free to take whatever they wanted. Nor is it clear what 'price' the Bolsheviks are supposed to have received. The German suggestion that a settlement which involved the truncation of vast areas of Russian territory was in some way an act of goodwill is no less difficult to believe.

Cartoon 14.5 Zum 3ten März 1918. *Fliegende Blätter,* Munich, 5.iv.1918

Cartoon 14.6 Eine nette Pflanze! *Kladderadatsch,* Berlin, 17.iii.1918

Eine nette Pflanze!

Mutter Austria: „Was willst Du denn noch, mein Liebling?"
Das unartige Ladisläuschen: „Cholm will ich haben und Danzig, sonst macht mir der ganze Weltkrieg keinen Spaß!"

This German cartoon comments on a side-effect of one of the Brest–Litovsk treaties: not the main treaty with Russia, but the treaty which had been concluded a few weeks earlier with the Ukraine. The town Cholm (Chelm; Kholm), which the Poles regarded as truly Polish, had been included in the Russian Empire since the eighteenth-century partitions, but the treaty allocated it to the 'satellite' Ukrainian state.

Germany and Austria are seen as the parents of the little Polish boy, who clutches the insignia of the kingdom of Poland, and the sealed promise of autonomy given by the Central Powers. This time, however, Poland is very far from being the contented boy of Cartoon 8.3, which had appeared in the same magazine fifteen months earlier. 'Mother Austria' asks 'the badly behaved little Ladislas' what he wants. He replies, 'I want to have Cholm and Danzig (Gdansk), otherwise the world war is no fun anymore!' The expression of German father suggests that he is not in an indulgent mood, and he evidently contemplates using the birch on the wall for corporal punishment of the spoilt, ungrateful and truculent child.

The interest of 'Ladislas' in Danzig seems to have had a different root, Danzig had been annexed by Prussia at the time of the partitions, but had an overwhelmingly German population. The Poles, however, were deeply concerned that the Polish state should have a good port, and President Wilson's Fourteen Points, which will be considered in the next chapter, had already been promulgated by the date of this cartoon, and proposed that Poland should become independent and should have access to the sea. If the Allies were prepared to allot a port to the Poles, the Poles were bound to set what pressure they could on the Central Powers to make a similar offer.

Cartoon 14.7 Das japanische Gespenst. *Fliegende Blätter,* Munich, 19.iv.1918

Das japanische Gespenst.

This cartoon shows a German view of the Japanese intervention in Siberia, a few weeks after the Treaty of Brest–Litovsk.

'The Japanese spectre' is a new version of 'the Yellow Peril' which had appalled some Europeans, including the Kaiser, at the turn of the century. The Japanese warrior with drawn sword rises from the waters, mounted on the Chinese dragon. Uncle Sam, John Bull, and a Frenchman stand on the shore, terrified at the apparition.

Cartoon 14.8 At the Kaiser's back door. *New York World*, New York, 11.viii.1918.

AT THE KAISER'S BACK DOOR.

In the summer of 1918, Allied intervention in Russia became more extensive, and troops were landed at Murmansk and Archangel. The primary object of these landings was to deny supplies to the Central Powers and to render assistance to the various 'white' forces who were fighting the Bolsheviks, and who were considered likely to revive the war against Germany.

In this American cartoon, Lenin is the tethered watchdog who guards 'the Kaiser's back door' against the advancing Allied soldiers. In truth Lenin had no interest at all in helping the Germans against the Allies, or *vice versa*, but both lots of belligerents insisted on seeing everything in terms of the conflict which immediately concerned them.

120

Cartoon 14.9 Der russische Klumpen Unglück.
Der Brummer, Berlin, 20.viii.1918.

Der russische Klumpen Unglück.   Die Alliierten: „Wir haben den Teig gut angesäuert, jetzt gärt er."

This German cartoon comments on the sheer anarchy and confusion which was developing in Russia in the late summer of 1918. The Allies are bakers who declare, 'We have yeasted the dough well, and now it's fermenting.' From the 'Russian lump of misery', various factions who were competing in different places and in different combinations are appearing: Bolsheviki, Mensheviki, Trudoviki, Tartu Social Revolutionaries, Cadets, Amur Cossacks, Czecho–Slovaks. Other shapes represent the State railways, State papers, and the Church, which in various ways provided further issues of contention.

15

The last throw

Once peace had been concluded between Germany and Russia at Brest–Litovsk, there was a realistic possibility that Germany could switch forces from the eastern front in time to deliver a knock-out blow at the Allies before Americans could arrive in great numbers.

It would take some time to move armies from the East on to the Western Front, and the nature of the ground would not encourage much action before the spring was well advanced. A major German offensive in the spring could be predicted with reasonable confidence, and on the success or failure of that offensive the outcome of the war was likely to be decided. As for the Allies, they had little reason for launching costly offensives until the Americans were able to take part. Several German attacks were made from late March onwards, but it was in May that they became most intense and most dangerous.

There were important developments in other directions during the first half of 1918. Early in January President Wilson proclaimed the Fourteen Points which he regarded as necessary for peace. These mentioned general objectives, including open international treaties, freedom of navigation on the high seas, the reduction of international trade barriers and the reduction of national armaments. There were also various specific objectives including the evacuation of occupied territories, and territorial changes (some of them vaguely stated) at the expense of the various Central Powers. The last two of Wilson's Points would prove particularly important in time to come: 'an independent Polish state . . . [with] secure access to the sea . . .' and 'a general association of nations . . . affording mutual guarantees . . . for great and small States alike.'

In later months the Fourteen Points were often seen, both in Allied countries and in the Central Powers, as an authoritative declaration of Allied war aims and as such they were to acquire great significance in the last phase of the war and in the aftermath.

Cartoon 15.1 Now, please hush! *New York Herald*, New York, 10.i.1918

NOW, PLEASE HUSH!

This cartoon shows an American reaction to the Fourteen Points proclaimed by President Wilson in January 1918. The Fourteen Points – the cartoonist suggested – constituted the Allied war aims, and should stop the German parrot (who wears the familiar moustache of the Kaiser) from complaining that these terms are unknown.

Unfortunately, this was a heavy over-simplification of the position. How far Wilson was able to commit his own country became increasingly doubtful as time went on, while he certainly could not commit the other Allies. Those Allies were so dependent on American assistance for any prospect of victory that they did not care to contradict the President, and many of their publicists eagerly supported his proposals, but it was by no means certain that their governments would be willing to follow the Fourteen Points when and if victory were achieved.

Cartoon 15.2 Growing downwards. *Liverpool Courier,* copied in *New Zealand Herald,* Auckland, 11.v.1918

GROWING DOWNWARDS.

As this cartoon indicates, the German propsects of U-boat victory were diminishing rapidly in the spring of 1918. A combination of the convoy system and the use of surface vessels to destroy U-boats had greatly reduced the risk to Britain from that direction. Any prospect of a German victory could only come from a successful attack by land.

Cartoon 15.3 Unsere Kriegskarte. *Kladderadatsch*, Berlin, 5.v.1918

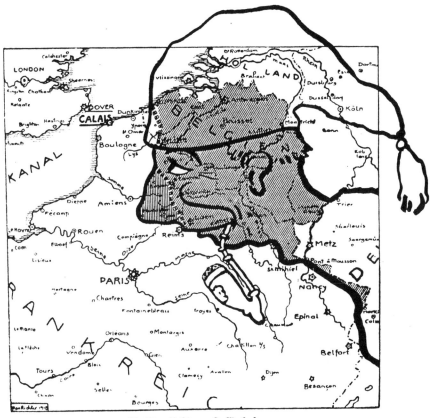

Unsere Kriegskarte

mit Aussicht auf Calais.

This German cartoon of early May 1918 neatly draws the line of battle on the Western Front as the head of 'Michel', 'with prospect of Calais'. If the Germans could control the Channel ports this might prove of crucial importance in cutting off British, and eventually American, supplies of men and material for France.

Cartoon 15.4 Remarques-tu Fritz? . . . *Le Journal,* Paris, 18.vi.1918

— Remarques-tu, Fritz, que nos officiers ont tout d'un coup cessé de nous dire : *Nach Paris?*

(Dessin de PALLIER.)

By mid-June 1918, this French cartoon was able to record with some confidence that the greatest threat of the German spring offensive had passed. One German soldier casually remarks to a friend, 'Do you notice, Fritz, that our officers have suddenly stopped saying to us, "On to Paris"?'

Cartoon 15.5 Discipline. *Punch*, London, 24.iv.1918

DISCIPLINE.

CARL HAPSBURG. "PLEASE, SIR, I DIDN'T WRITE IT."

DR. HOHENZOLLERN. "FOR THE CREDIT OF THE SCHOOL I SHALL PUBLICLY ACCEPT YOUR DENIAL. ALL THE SAME, MY BOY, YOU WILL NOW STEP INTO MY PRIVATE ROOM."

Early in April 1918, the French government published correspondence which, it claimed, had been written a year earlier by the Austro–Hungarian Emperor Karl to his brother-in-law Prince Sixte of Bourbon–Parma. The Prince was encouraged to tell Poincaré of Austria–Hungary's willingness, *inter alia*, to support 'the French just claim in regard to Alsace–Lorraine' in the event of peace negotiations. When the French statement was published, Karl indignantly denied its accuracy.

In this cartoon 'Dr Hohenzollern', the stern headmaster, expresses force-fully his own reservations on 'Karl Habsburg's' denial.

16

Collapse, 1918

When the German offensive on the Western Front petered out in the early summer of 1918, the outcome of the war was in one sense decided. In any settlement which would eventually emerge, the Allies would have the upper hand, although the measure of their dominance and the form of the settlement which would emerge were by no means predetermined. In the knowledge that American troops were already arriving, and would continue to arrive in great numbers, the Allies were disposed to ignore the various pleas for peace negotiations. The longer they waited, the clearer and more decisive their dominance would be.

Bulgaria was the weakest of the Central Powers, and was the first to collapse. The Allied position at Salonika, which for most of the war had seemed a wasteful disposition of many soldiers, suddenly acquired importance. In September 1918, combined efforts from troops of several of the Allied countries in the vicinity of the Vardar valley led to a general retreat of the Bulgarian forces. On 30 September, Bulgaria obtained an armistice on adverse terms, and a few days later King Ferdinand abdicated in favour of his son.

Turkey was now completely cut off from contact with the other Central Powers. There was some delay, apparently because the country's rulers saw merit in the Central Powers seeking peace collectively. In the early part of October, a combination of Allied troops and Arab rebels cleared most of the Levant from Ottoman control. The politicians who had been most closely associated with the war policy resigned about this time, and at the end of the month Turkey obtained an armistice. There was, however, no great immediate change in the political organisation of the country. Sultan Mehmet V had died in July, but his brother and successor, sixth of the name, would remain on the throne for a considerable time to come.

Austria–Hungary had been actively concerned with the promotion of peace negotiations ever since the closing weeks of 1916. Not only was defeat certain to bring disaster, but even victory offered little prospect of reward, as the Brest–Litovsk settlement had shown. In the course of 1918 matters acquired an increasing urgency, as the Habsburg state began gradually to fall apart.

It has been seen that many pro-Allied Czechs and Slovaks had been fighting in Russia for a long time. Others had found their way to America or Western Europe, and in August 1918 the Allies formally recognised the Czechoslovaks as an Allied government. For the time being there was little which had much claim to be regarded as a veritable Czech state, but by the end of September a Czechoslovak National Council had come into existence in Prague, and a month later had largely taken over the functions of government.

Parallel developments were taking place among the South Slav subjects of the Empire. There was even one curious anticipation of an inter-Allied dispute which became important a few months later. Towards the end of October, the Adriatic port of Fiume (now Rijeka) was seized by Croats. Perhaps they were at least as anxious to hold the town against future Italian claims as to assert Croatian independence from the Empire.

The Emperor himself was by no means averse to national development. In the middle of October, Karl proposed that the 'Austrian' part of the Empire should become a federal state organised on national lines, and appeared willing to cede the Polish territories of Galicia to an independent Poland. Before the month was out Hungary had become virtually a separate state. At the very beginning of November, 'German Austria' – that is, Austria in the modern sense of the term – had been taken over by a state council, which sought admission to the German Federation. Not long afterwards the German districts of Bohemia, nucleus of the 'Sudetenland' which would attract so much attention in 1938, sought to break away from Czech Bohemia.

In the middle of September 1918, the Austro–Hungarian government sent notes to all belligerents, calling on them to investigate whether a basis for peace existed, but this approach was rejected by the Allies. By late October peace was being sought independently of Germany.

At last, on 3 November 1918, an armistice was concluded between what remained of Austria–Hungary and the Allies, which was to take effect on the following day. The various nationalities within the disintegrating Empire all hoped to escape full Allied wrath in the peace settlement, and separated themselves as rapidly as they could from the vestige of the Habsburg state. Finally, on 12 November, Karl abdicated – perhaps the most sincere peace-lover of all the heads of state on either side.

In Germany the process of collapse followed a rather different course. Early in October 1918 Prince Max of Baden became Imperial Chancellor and Foreign Minister of Prussia. A significant political development was that two Socialists were appointed Secretaries of State at the same time. On 12 October, Germany indicated willingness to accept peace on the basis of the 'Fourteen Points' which President Wilson had promulgated in January.

On 3 November – the day of the Austro–Hungarian armistice – there was a mutiny of the German fleet at Kiel. This was followed swiftly by the establishment of Councils of Workmen's and Soldiers' Delegates in most of the large towns. Bavaria followed a course of its own and on 7 November a republic was proclaimed, headed by the socialist journalist Kurt Eisner. For some time there was uncertainty as to how far Bavaria could still properly be considered part of Germany at all.

On 8 November German plenipotentiaries at last received armistice terms from Marshal Foch, with the requirement that these be accepted within three days. On 9 November Max of Baden resigned and a socialist, Friedrich Ebert, became Chancellor in his place. On the same day the abdication of Wilhelm II was announced, and on the next day he fled to the Netherlands. Then, at 5 a.m. on 11 November, armistice terms were signed, and six hours later hostilities ceased.

Although the fighting was over, it was still very far from clear to anybody what kind of peace settlement might be expected to emerge.

Cartoon 16.1 L'Intruse. *Le Canard Enchaîné,* Paris, 17.vii.1918

L'INTRUSE

-- *Vos papiers ?*
.— *Des papiers, moi ? Vous ne m'avez pas regardée ?... Je suis la Grippe Espagnole...*

In the summer and autumn of 1918 a particularly virulent form of influenza, usually known as 'Spanish 'flu', appeared in Europe and soon in other continents as well. The mortality was high, and the disease seemed particularly prevalent and severe among young and apparently healthy people. While it would be difficult to argue that this visitation was of crucial importance for the course of the war, it may have been one of the factors affecting the ability of armies to fight.

In this French cartoon, 'the intruder' is challenged unsuccessfully for her authorisation or passport papers at the Franco-Spanish frontier.

Cartoon 16.2 One support knocked away.
Rand Daily Mail, Johannesburg, 2.x.1918

ONE SUPPORT KNOCKED AWAY.

This South African cartoon from early October 1918 comments on the Bulgarian military collapse and subsequent armistice which took place at the end of the previous month, through a military operation in which troops of several countries were involved. The 'entente' – i.e., the Allies – strike away King Ferdinand of Bulgaria, one of the supports of the German warrior, who is thereby destabilised. Another support, the Turk, regards the situation with apprehension. Several Allied cartoons use a different image to mark the Bulgarian defection: a rat leaving a sinking ship.

132

Cartoon 16.3 Trouble in the asylum. *London Opinion,*
London, 12.x.1918

TROUBLE IN THE ASYLUM.

This British cartoon sees the Bulgarian escape from the 'Germanic lunatic asylum' as the forerunner of more defections. Turkey, followed closely by Austria, prepares to do the same. 'Keeper Wilhelm' shows concern at the proceedings.

Cartoon 16.4 A bogus note. *New York Times,* New York, 13.x.1918

"THAT SIGNATURE IS NO GOOD; HAVE THE LADY SIGN IT."

On 12 October the German government offered to accept peace on terms of President Wilson's Fourteen Points. This American cartoon appeared on the following day. The new German Chancellor, Prince Max of Baden, tenders to the 'paying teller' President Wilson a cheque for 'peace' signed by Wilhelm II. Wilson refuses the cheque, insisting that 'the lady' – Germany – must sign it. The implication seems to be that the Kaiser must go before peace, or even armistice, terms can be considered.

Cartoon 16.5 Kamarad républicain. *La Victoire*, Paris, 10.xi.1918

KAMARAD RÉPUBLICAIN   par HERMANN-PAUL

, — Fritz, ton bonnet ne t'empêche pas d'avoir les mains sales...

On 9 November 1918 the socialist Friedrich Ebert became Chancellor of Germany, and on the same day the abdication of the Kaiser was announced. In this French cartoon 'Fritz', the German soldier, wears the Phrygian cap of liberty and lifts his hands in surrender. The Allied soldiers, however, insist that his headgear does not stop him having dirty hands. The implication is that his past misdeeds will not be forgiven because he has recently set up a democratic regime.

17

Aftermath

The various armistice arrangements reached in the autumn of 1918 left no doubt that the Allies had been victorious, but they fell far short of unconditional surrender and there remained, in theory, a possibility that fighting might be renewed.

In practice, however, the armistice arrangements made this impossible from a military point of view. All of the armistices required measures of demobilisation, the surrender of much military and naval equipment, the evacuation of occupied territory, and also the evacuation of territory to which specific Allies had long laid unambiguous claims, such as Alsace–Lorraine, and some of the areas of Austria–Hungary demanded by Italy. Germany was also required to evacuate the Rhineland, an area of great strategic importance lying between the Franco–German frontier and the Rhine, with a few bridgeheads east of the river. The occupations and re-occupations of liberated and coveted lands were accompanied by all the predictable scenes of public drama and popular enthusiasm. Those who did not like what was happening no doubt stayed at home.

There were no political requirements. Kaiser Wilhelm II had already abdicated and fled his country when the German armistice was made, King Ferdinand of Bulgaria and the Emperor Karl of Austria–Hungary remained on their thrones for a few days after their respective armistices, Sultan Mehmet VI for several years. Austria–Hungary was already disintegrating at the time of the relevant armistice, but there was no requirement by terms of the armistice that the process of disintegration should continue.

Before November was out great changes had already taken place. Not only the two Emperors but the hereditary sovereigns of the various German states had been driven out. The break-up of Austria–Hungary was complete. Only a few days after fighting ceased, the new Czech state was sufficiently organised to appoint a definite government. The Polish state had been proclaimed early in the month. Once the Central Powers were disarmed, Poles occupied the Polish districts of Germany and Austria–Hungary. The most serious military problem which the Poles met was not opposition from forces of the erstwhile Central Powers, but resistance from Ukrainians in ethnically mixed districts of Eastern Galicia.

The term Yugoslavia (usually spelt with a J at that date) was already coming into use. At the time of the dissolution of Austria–Hungary the name was used for a provisional administration of South Slavs which was set up at Agram (Zagreb), and which seemed to favour friendly relations with the Serbs. There were many questions at issue between the southern Slavs from within and outside the former dual monarchy. Relations between different kinds of South Slavs were not always good. Then, late in November, a further complication arose. A congress with dubious authority, meeting at Podgoritza, passed a resolution deposing King Nicholas of Montenegro, and uniting his country with Serbia. A considerable period would elapse before that issue, and the general framework of the future Yugoslavian kingdom, was agreed.

Some very important developments occurred in major Allied countries during the last two months of 1918. A few days before the German armistice the United States held a set of Congressional Elections, as the country's constitution prescribed. The result was a substantial swing towards President Wilson's Republican opponents who secured majorities in both Houses: a matter which would prove of high importance a few months later.

In Britain, where the rules about election dates are more lax, the Armistice was followed almost immediately by a General Election. The ordinary rules, indeed, would have prescribed an election not later than the end of 1915, but Parliament had prolonged its own life year by year during the war. Not long before the Armistice, important electoral changes had been introduced. In place of the old 'Household Franchise', practically every male received a vote at age 21. Women received a vote for the first time, but at age 30. The truly remarkable character of the election will be considered in the light of cartoons; suffice it here to say that Lloyd George's Coalition Government was returned with a great majority, but the political 'centre of gravity' of the Parliament which supported it changed greatly.

In Germany there was widespread famine in the aftermath of the war, but what food there was seems to have been distributed fairly. The predominantly Social-Democratic government of Ebert which had been formed shortly before the Armistice encountered much violence from extremists, some of whom regarded the Russian Bolsheviks as a model. In January 1919, however, elections to the new National Assembly resulted in a large majority for what might be termed the moderate left, with the Social Democrats by far the largest single party, though well short of an overall majority. A few weeks later, Ebert was elected first President of the German Republic. Although Bavaria remained in turmoil for some time to come, it looked as if most of Germany had settled – for the time being at least – into the forms of a parliamentary democracy.

Like Germany itself, the rump of 'German Austria' which remained after the dissolution of the Austro–Hungarian Empire experienced starvation, particularly in Vienna. The country held an election in February 1919, with results not wildly different from those in Germany. Indications suggest that most people would have preferred to join Germany, although the tiny western province of Vorarlberg would have preferred to join Switzerland.

The Allies, however, whatever their protestations about rights of self-determination, were unwilling to apply those precepts to people of German language and culture. Even before the peace treaties were promulgated, it was abundantly clear that no kind of union between Germany and Austria would be permitted, and later the Swiss decided that it was prudent to refuse admission to Vorarlberg. The German-speaking parts of Bohemia were compelled by force of arms to remain in Czechoslovakia, while the South Tyrol – the northern part which spoke German, as well as the southern part which spoke Italian – had been promised to Italy as part of the price of Italian support in the war. By the same token, nobody dreamed of asking the people of Alsace and Lorraine whether they wished to belong to Germany or France.

The fate of the Hungarian section of the Habsburg Empire was little better than that of the old Austrian part. The south Slav part of the Lands of St Stephen had passed to the incipient Yugoslavia. Romanians established themselves in Transylvania, Czechs in Slovakia. No distinction was made between the truly Magyar parts of those lands and the parts which were of mixed nationality. In March 1919, a regime with ideas close to those of the Russian Bolsheviks was installed, and it was not removed until the following August.

Bulgaria seems at first sight to have been let off comparatively lightly. The armistice terms naturally required her to evacuate occupied Greek and Serb territory, but she was not required at this stage to relinquish territory to hostile occupation, save where this was required for military operations. No doubt to the Bulgars' relief, it was the major Allies, not the other Balkan states, who were allowed to perform that occupation. The apparent generosity of these terms, however, seems less impressive when it is recalled that Bulgaria had been on the losing side in the Second Balkan War of 1913, and her victorious neighbours had already seized all that they required.

The immediate requirements imposed by the Ottoman armistice were largely strategic; but Turkish troops remaining in the Arab lands and Libya were required to surrender. It was evident from the start that those territories would be passed over to the Allies, or to pro-Allied local regimes. Special provisions were made in the 'Six Vilayets' where – prior to the massacres – Armenians had formed a large part of the population. These were evidently designed mainly to protect the remnant of that unhappy people.

The overall picture of the former belligerents in the immediate after-math of the various armistices was fairly clear. The original Wilsonian doctrine of 'peace without annexations' had been completely forgotten, and the more recent doctrine of the Fourteen Points would be – at best – of limited application. Broadly speaking, the major Allies immediately secured *de facto* control of whatever territory they coveted, for themselves or for their satellites, subject only to the qualification that they might later dispute some of that territory among themselves. In other lands which had formerly belonged to the Central Powers, regimes sympathetic with the Allies were encouraged to carve out nation-states. The principle of nationality was sacred where it operated in favour of the Allies, but where it operated in the other direction it could be brushed aside. There was recognition that 'Bolshevism' really did present a serious threat in some places, and some people issued solemn warnings about the general nature of that threat; but governments of the former Central Powers were left to their own devices in controlling 'Bolshevism', with scant assistance, economic or military, from the Allies.

Cartoon 17.1 The vital points! *John Bull,* London, 14.xii.1918

THE VITAL POINTS!

Pinning Them Down!

John Bull was a weekly periodical aimed at a largely working-class readership. Its politics were sometimes radical, but always arrogantly nationalist. 'The vital points' expresses a simplistic and vindictive view of what is required.

'The return of Odysseus' is a German cartoon which appeared about five weeks after the Armistice. It sets a different political interpretation on events and is anxious, but certainly not despairing, in its message. The young German soldier returning home is cast as Odysseus, 'Germania' as his faithful wife, Penelope. She is beset unwillingly by suitors, as in the original story. In this case, all but one are socialists of one kind or another. Karl Liebknecht was the revolutionary 'Spartacist' leader, Kurt Eisner had set up the short-lived socialist republic of Bavaria. Friedrich Ebert, the Chancellor, was soon to become first President of the German Republic, Hugo Haase, an Independent Socialist, was associated with Ebert's original Supreme Council, formed a couple of days before the Armistice, Mathias Erzberger was a left-wing member of the Catholic Zentrum – an

Cartoon 17.2 Die Heimkehr des Odysseus.
Kladderadatsch, Berlin, 15.xii.1918

Die Heimkehr des Odysseus

advocate of the League of Nations idea well before the end of the war, who led the German delegation which signed the armistice.

It is a reflection on the turbulent condition of Germany at the time that four of the five men would soon come to violent ends. Liebknecht was killed in January 1919, Eisner in February, and Haase towards the end of the year. Erzberger was assassinated in 1921.

Cartoon 17.3 'To hell with party politics!' *World,* New York, 7.xi.1918

"TO HELL WITH PARTY POLITICS!"

This American cartoon was drawn just after results of the Congressional elections of November 1918 were declared. The cartoonist's message is evidently that 'party politics' are unimportant by comparison with the continuing war. The view, however, was completely unrealistic. The war was virtually over, and 'party politics' would play an enormous part in determining what would happen in the aftermath.

President Wilson's Democratic Party suffered serious defeat. In both Houses, control passed from the Democrats to the Republicans. The change in political outlook which this implied was to have a great effect on American attitudes to international affairs.

Cartoon 17.4 Camouflaged. *Westminster Gazette*, London, 2.i.1919

A TORY DESTROYER.

CAMOUFLAGED.

This *Westminster Gazette* cartoon comments bitterly on the results of the British General Election of December 1918, which had recently been declared.

The conditions of the election were extraordinary. Prime Minister Lloyd George had hoped to broaden the Coalition over which he presided in the second half of the war, by incorporating the 'Asquithian' wing of the Liberal Party as well as his own section, while he appears to have believed that the Labour Party would remain in the government.

As it happened, the pattern of events was completely different. Asquith refused to join the Coalition and Labour withdrew from it. Thus the government supporters were for practical purposes the Conservatives and a section of the Liberals, plus a small group of 'oddments'. The Coalition won a huge majority; but, inevitably, the Conservatives predominated greatly over the Lloyd George Liberals within that Coalition.

The cartoonist was an Asquithian Liberal, shocked by the defeat sustained by his own chief and most of Asquith's followers. Recollecting the camouflage of vessels used during the war, he sees the government as a 'Tory destroyer', carrying the face and name of Lloyd George as a mere camouflage. The results of that General Election were bound to exert an important influence on international as well as domestic events.

Cartoon 17.5 The first German victory. *Punch*, London, 29.i.1919

THE FIRST GERMAN VICTORY.

[The German Elections have resulted in a signal defeat for the Extremists.]

In the immediate aftermath of the fighting 'Bolshevism' came to occupy the sort of place in everyone's demonology which 'the enemy' had held a few months earlier. Most cartoons in both Allied and ex-enemy countries portray Bolshevism as a great force of evil – often as a wolf, which in those days was commonly thought to be a particularly malevolent animal.

This British cartoon of January 1919 commemorates the German General Election of that month, which resulted in heavy defeat for political forces in the country which might be called 'Bolshevik'. This is one of the few Allied cartoons of the period in which the Germans are seen sympathetically.

18

A sort of peace

The process of bringing the war to a formal conclusion was long and bitter, involving savage disputes at all levels: within the separate countries, Allied or Central Power; between the various Allies; between the Allies and the defeated enemy. No pretence was made that the body reaching the decisions was a Congress of all Great Powers, like the Congresses which resolved the Napoleonic War in 1815, the Crimean War in 1856, or the Russo–Turkish War in 1878. The victorious Allies met in Paris to decide what terms they proposed to impose, and then report those terms to the vanquished. Thereafter they would listen to specific arguments from the defeated, but in the end the enemy would be required to comply with orders.

Several Central Powers were involved and separate treaties were made, but the treaty which attracted by far the most attention was what eventually became the Treaty of Versailles with Germany. While the settlement was being debated the terrible blockade of Germany continued, even though the other blockades were eventually relaxed. How many Germans died as a result of that blockade between the armistice and the Treaty of Versailles is arguable, but there seems little doubt that the number must be enormous.

During the Allied debates an issue not directly connected with the German settlement at all nearly wrecked the conference. The Italians, relying on their own interpretation of the secret Treaty of London which had enticed them into the war in 1915, wrangled bitterly with the French, and to some extent the British, over claims to former Austro–Hungarian territory in the Adriatic region, which France proposed to give to the incipient Yugoslavia. The United States had not been a party to the 1915 treaty, but tended to side with the French and British. At one point the Italians left the Conference, and it seemed that peace would have to be made without them. In the end the Italians backed down, but the fate of the town of Fiume was not settled until 1924. There were also bitter disputes between Japan and China about the reversion of German interests in the Far East.

In the end the Allies more or less resolved their differences, and on 7 May 1919 Clémenceau presented the German representatives with the

Allied demands. Much was predictable: loss of the German colonies, loss of Alsace–Lorraine to France, loss of the 'Polish Corridor': a strip of Polish land which was thrust between the bulk of Germany and the eastern part of Prussia, and reached the sea at Gdynia. There would be other important territorial losses as well. A great indemnity would be required, but the sum was not yet fixed. The German army was to be greatly reduced, and most of the navy handed over to the Allies. What particularly shocked the Germans was the 'war guilt' clause, which effectively set upon Germany and her associates sole responsibility for the war and its consequences.

The original Allied demand was that Germany should raise whatever questions or criticisms she might have of these terms in fifteen days, but eventually the period dragged on to six weeks. A few small modifications were made, but on 16 June, the Germans were required to accept or reject the terms in their entirety within five days.

Many Germans wished to refuse. There was no way in which they could resume the war, but they could leave the Allies to occupy all Germany and impose what terms they required on the supine people. Arguably that solution would have been best for all concerned, Allies and Germans alike. The German Chancellor thought so, and resigned when that view was not accepted by his colleagues. On 28 June, the Treaty of Versailles was signed. So far as Germany was concerned, the war was over.

There remained the question of Germany's allies. Who should speak for the former Austria–Hungary? The state had ceased to exist. Three whole countries had been formed from the remains of the Empire, and for practical purposes the remainder had been annexed by four other countries.

Treatment of the Austro–Hungarian successors was wildly disparate. Austria and Hungary were both treated as defeated enemies, although their combined population was well under a third of the total population of the Empire. Czechoslovakia, whose population was not very different from those two combined, was treated as an honoured ally, although the country was barely in existence when the war ended.

A draft treaty was presented to Austria at St Germain on 2 June. As with Germany, there were long negotiations, and the treaty was not finally signed until September. The essential features of the treaty had been adumbrated months earlier, in the arrangements permitted by the Allies in the immediate aftermath of the armistice. The South Tyrol (Alto Adige) would pass to Italy, while the German-speaking Austrians of Bohemia were required to remain in Czechoslovakia, Vorarlberg would not be allowed to pass to Switzerland, nor would the rump of 'German Austria' be permitted to join Germany. St Germain, even more than Versailles, supported the view that high-sounding principles like the Fourteen Points might apply to others, but not to people of German speech.

The other peace treaties were framed in a similar spirit. Bulgaria was perhaps the most fortunate of the former Central Powers; by the Treaty of Neuilly, in November 1919, she lost some territory to Greece and Yugoslavia, but the bulk of the country remained intact. By contrast, the Treaty of Trianon reduced Hungary to but a quarter of pre-war size, and every one of her neighbours – even Austria – gained Hungarian territory. In August the Treaty of Sèvres reduced the Ottoman Empire to an even smaller proportion of its former dimensions.

Not all was settled yet, by a long way. The western limits of the Soviet Union were not defined until 1921. The Treaty of Sèvres, far from producing even a temporary settlement, led swiftly to a new war with the Greeks, and it was not until 1923 that the Treaty of Lausanne imposed more durable arrangements. It would extend the range of this book too much to discuss all those treaties and the conditions which accompanied them in the light of contemporary cartoons.

In any event, Versailles was from every point of view by far the most important of the peace treaties. Germany was still a large and important country, even in defeat, while Austria, Hungary, Bulgaria and Turkey were not. It was very clear indeed that Versailles was almost unanimously resented in Germany. The treaty could only be maintained if either it were modified in a manner which would make it acceptable – or, in the alternative, if the major ex-Allies were prepared to act together, by war if necessary, to enforce the Versailles arrangements throughout the whole future. Probably before 1919 was out, and certainly by the end of 1920, it was clear that the United States had no intention of joining in such action. Italy was already deeply aggrieved by the peace treaty arrangements, and in the course of the next few years a great wedge would be driven between Britain and France. Many people in all countries were terrified of the new Russia, and what action she would take in the matter was anybody's guess.

Victory in the 'war to end war' had turned to dust and ashes.

Cartoon 18.1 Das Denkmal ... *Der Brummer*, Berlin, No.3 (about January), 1919

Das Denkmal, das sich die Entente gesetzt hat.

Within a very short time, the mixture of curiosity and hope which existed in the Central Powers at the moment of the armistice had turned to bitter cynicism about the future.

This German cartoon, 'The monument which the entente has built for itself', expresses that cynicism cogently. On the pedestal of Uncle Sam is the word 'Justice'; but the bag of dollars in one pan of his scales outweighs the heart in the other. John Bull has the word 'Freedom' on his pedestal, but he encircles the ships with a chain. The tiger – Clémenceau – slavers for prey, but the word on his pedestal is 'Humanity'. The King of Italy fishes in his pond for all that he can get, but the word on the pedestal is 'Unselfishness'.

The message of this 'monument' in current circumstances is that financial considerations outweigh human feeling with the United States; that Britain proclaims freedom of the seas, but is still playing the leading part in blockading (and starving) Germany; that France hungers for revenge; and that Italy is preoccupied with selfish interests.

Cartoon 18.2 Der bertrogene Betrüger. *Kladderadatsch*, Berlin, 11.v.1919

Der betrogene Betrüger

Judas=Emanuel: „Weih, o weih! Sie wollen mir meine 30 Silberlinge nicht geben!"

This German cartoon, 'The betrayed betrayer' comments cyncially on the deep disputes between victors at the Paris Peace Conference which met early in 1919.

Clémenceau, Lloyd George and (apparently) Wilson are cast as the chief priests of Israel, Victor Emmanuel III as Judas Iscariot. The cartoon, however, departs substantially from the Bible story, for the chief priests here refuse Judas the thirty pieces of silver – two of them named Fiume and the Adriatic region – for his betrayal.

German bitterness against the Italian decision to enter the war on the Allied side, which seemed to be in violation of that country's obligations under the old Triple Alliance, had been intense, and this cartoon suggests that Italy was still not forgiven. The French were currently anxious to assist their Balkan ally, the future Yugoslavia, which was being established. When the draft peace arrangements indicated that Italy would fail to gain the town of Fiume and extensive parts of the Adriatic coast, this caused huge indignation in Italy and at one point seemed to threaten the peace conference itself.

Cartoon 18.3 Madame Germania ... *Le Journal,* Paris, 16.v.1919

   -- *Madame Germania, je vous rends le petit livre que vous m'avez prêté il y a 48 ans. :*   (Dessin de JEAN ROUTIER.)

This French cartoon appeared shortly after the original draft of the peace treaty with Germany was published. The settlement is seen as a simple act of revenge for the injustice done by Prussia/Germany on France in 1871. Marianne returns to 'Madame Germania' 'the little book' – the peace treaty – which had been loaned to her forty-eight years earlier.

Cartoon 18.4 On n'est jamais ... *Le Canard Enchaîné*,
Paris, 21.v.1919

ON N'EST JAMAIS TROP PRUDENT.

Les « Voyages Duchemin » organisent
des excursions en automobiles pour visiter les champs de bataille.
(LES JOURNAUX)

Dites-moi, chauffeur, vous êtes bien sûr que la guerre est terminée ?

For a time there was serious doubt whether Germany would sign the peace treaty proposed for her by the Allies.

This cartoon, 'You can never be too careful', links the debate with the recent decision of a commercial organisation to arrange motor tours of the battlefields. The prospective passenger asks the driver whether he is really sure that the war is over.

Is the taxi perhaps an oblique reference to the celebrated occasion when French troops were driven to the front in Paris taxis?

153

Cartoon 18.5 A strong inducement to sign. *Bulletin,*
Glasgow, 20.vi.1919

A STRONG INDUCEMENT TO SIGN

This Scottish cartoon makes no secret of the fact that Germany is being
compelled to make peace at pistol point, with no sort of objective enquiry
into the merits of the matter. A German cartoon in *Kladderadatsch* a little
later uses a similar, but even more dramatic image. Michel signs the
' "Just" Peace of the Entente' with a pistol pointed at his head, while the
Devil grins at the proceedings.

Cartoon 18.6 Il trattato di pace. *Avanti*, Milan, 14.v.1919

Il trattato di pace

Madri, preparate dell'altra carne da cannone!

This Italian cartoon appeared in a critical periodical shortly after the Allied peace terms were published. The message at the bottom is grimly prophetic. 'Mothers! Prepare more cannon fodder!' is a loose translation. The stormy scene outside the window suggests the turbulent world which awaits the baby.

Cartoon 18.7 The head of the firm. *World*, New York, 12.ix.1919

THE HEAD OF THE FIRM

These two American cartoons both appeared on 12 September 1919. Most of the peace treaties had still not been concluded, but already the question of future American relations with former European Allies had become a matter of intense controversy in the United States.

When Wilson presented the Treaty of Versailles to the Senate for ratification, a small minority of Senators opposed the President's proposal in its entirety. A much more formidable group of critics was led by Senator Henry Cabot Lodge, Chairman of the Republican-dominated Foreign Affairs Committee, who was deeply opposed to the President's view that the United States should play a leading role in the new League of Nations. The New York *World* takes a very bitter view of Lodge and the Republicans ('G.O.P.' = Grand Old Party); but the *San Francisco Chronicle*

Cartoon 18.8 The real quitter. *San Francisco Chronicle,* 12.ix.1919

suggests that Wilson himself had already jettisoned several of the famous Fourteen Points, and was therefore 'the real quitter'.

About three weeks after these cartoons appeared Wilson suffered a serious stroke. Its effects were not sufficiently grave to produce his retirement from office, but reduced his capacities considerably. In the following year, 1920, the Republican Warren G. Harding was elected as Wilson's successor. The United States did not ratify the Treaty of Versailles, but in 1921 signed a separate treaty of peace with Germany, specifically declaring that it would not be bound by those parts of the Versailles arrangements which related to the Covenant of the League of Nations. This marked the beginning of 'isolation', which dominated the country's foreign policy during the inter-war years.